Knowledge Without Goodness
Is Dangerous

John Phillips
Founder of Phillips Exeter Academy, 1781

From the portrait by Joseph Steward
Courtesy of Dartmouth College

Knowledge Without Goodness Is Dangerous

Moral Education in Boarding Schools

Edited by
Charles L. Terry

The Phillips Exeter Academy Press
1981

KNOWLEDGE WITHOUT GOODNESS IS DANGEROUS: MORAL EDUCATION IN BOARDING SCHOOLS. Copyright © 1981 by the Trustees of Phillips Exeter Academy. All rights reserved. Printed in the United States of America. No part of this book may be used or reproduced in any manner whatsoever without written permission except in the case of brief quotations embodied in critical notes and reviews. For information address The Phillips Exeter Academy Press, c/o the Director of Publications, Phillips Exeter Academy, Exeter, N.H. 03833.

Library of Congress Cataloging in Publication Data

Main entry under title:

Knowledge without goodness is dangerous.

    Chiefly pages from the Summer Institute on Moral Education, held June 18-30, 1978 at Phillips Exeter Academy.

    Bibliography: p.

    Contents: Moral education: provocations for an institute/Theodore Sizer —Summary of the first plenary session—Observations on three days of the Institute/Christopher M. Brookfield and David R. Weber/Moral Education and the culture of the school/Joseph Reimer/etc.

    1. Boarding schools/United States/Addresses, essays, lectures. 2. Moral education/United States/Addresses, essays, lectures. I. Terry, Charles L., 1931-
II. Phillips Exeter Academy. III. Summer Institute on Moral Education. (1978 : Phillips Exeter Academy)

LC49.K56   370.11'4   81-81105

ISBN 0-939618-00-1   AACR2

02 03 04 05 10 9 8 7 6 5 4 3

But above all, it is expected that the attention of instructors to the disposition of the minds and morals of the youth under their charge will exceed every other care; well considering that though goodness without knowledge is weak and feeble, yet knowledge without goodness is dangerous, and that both united form the noblest character; and lay the surest foundation of usefulness to mankind.

> John Phillips in the
> Original Deed of Gift,
> Phillips Exeter Academy, 1781

To the memory of
Henry Wilkinson Bragdon
and
Theodore Reilly Seabrooke, Jr.,
always moral educators

CONTENTS

	Preface	xi
I	Prologue	1
II	Moral Education: Provocations for an Institute (Theodore R. Sizer)	4
III	Summary of the First Plenary Session	13
IV	Observations on Three Days of the Institute (Christopher M. Brookfield and David R. Weber)	18
V	Moral Education and the Culture of the School (Joseph Reimer)	30
VI	Summary of Robert Kegan's Remarks	37
VII	Promoting Moral Action Through Moral Education (Joseph Reimer)	40
VIII	Summary of Lawrence Kohlberg's Opening Remarks	46
IX	Summary of Schools Presenting "What Do We Do Right?"	48
X	Response (Lawrence Kohlberg)	52
XI	Summary of Douglas Heath's Presentations	59
XII	Summary of Schools Presenting "What Will We Take Back in the Fall?"	67
XIII	Final Day of the Institute (Charles L. Terry; Joseph E. Fellows; Stephen G. Kurtz)	70
XIV	A Paper from the Institute (Harvard V. Knowles)	76
XV	The Residential School as a Moral Environment (Harvard V. Knowles and David R. Weber)	79
XVI	Notes from a Panel Discussion on Discipline (Stephen G. Kurtz)	88

XVII	Some Remarks on Moral Education (Charles L. Terry)	91
XVIII	Moral Education: An Essay (Charles L. Terry)	95
XIX	Epilogue	101
	Appendix	
	A. A Talk in Phillips Church, May, 1977 (Thomas W. Holcombe)	106
	B. Can Our Schools Teach Personal Morality? A Proposal for a Summer Institute for Teachers	112
	C. Participants, Resource Colleagues and Administrators: Summer Institute on Moral Education, June, 1978, Exeter, New Hampshire	117
	D. Memorandum to President Charles Dey and the Choate-Rosemary Hall Community (Charles P. Twichell)	118

PREFACE

This book is a Phillips Exeter Academy Bicentennial publication. While it is to a large extent a documented report of the first Bicentennial Summer Institute which was held at Exeter in June, 1978, it has a wider purpose: it is intended to represent one of the Academy's efforts to honor its founder's famous charge. If "moral education" sounds trendy or imprecise to us today, it is not likely that John Phillips would have objected to the phrase: his Calvinistic certainty would have enabled him to see clearly and distinctly what "moral education" ought to mean to those not jaded or cynical.

Those, like Lawrence Kohlberg, who have been scholars in the subject will argue the critical necessity of being precise about what one means by the phrase. But they are capacious enough of imagination to let the subject extend to a vision of the totality of the educational enterprise. Moral education leads one inevitably to a vision of integration: it is a synthesizing vision. "No one person," as Kohlberg wryly notes, "can be a combination of Socrates, Carl Rogers and Abraham Lincoln," but educators can profitably theorize about helping the young — and themselves — achieve an integration of what Pascal called the orders of "mind," "spirit," and "charity." We *do* believe the truism that education is a fulfillment of the whole person; nevertheless, we have become increasingly uncertain that the triple-threat model of teacher, residential counselor-adviser and coach — quaintly referred to as a "good schoolman" — is exclusively the model sufficient to our times. We must, of course, continue to demand practical competence of the highest order in our faculties, but we need urgently to have men and women in our schools of a philosophical bent, people who are committed to the principle that collegiality is ultimately realized not so much in a common practical experience as in a common vision of ideals. Confident in our practical skills and in our knowledge, we must go further and dare to prize reflection and self-examination. And if these activities are "theoretical," we must remember that what may be of enduring practical value in them is the process of reflection itself.

What is represented in these pages is a process of reflection so compelling that twenty-one faculty members, three from each of seven boarding schools, might have dreamed of setting themselves up as a faculty in their own school. When they left Exeter at the end of a two-week Institute, their spirits were high and their attitudes impressively complex: they felt both a sense of urgency to do something about the moral atmosphere of their respective schools *and* a conviction that fruitful change comes slowly, is the result of reflection, of careful self-examination.

That reflection and self-examination — to which Phillips Exeter Academy is especially dedicated in this Bicentennial year — reveals a healthy tension of ideas and attitudes, even, perhaps, a dialectic. Should we define "moral education" in the most precise terms or should we allow it to subsume the entirety of what boarding schools try to do? Should moral education be primarily didactic or should it be contextual, informing the myriad personal relationships that occur in such distinct communities? Should we emphasize an ethical approach to our students' development, seeking to make them autonomous, inner-directed human beings, or should we invoke a moral code to which they can worthily conform? Should we be eager to confront our colleagues honestly when we think they miseducate morally or should we create structures in our schools that will augment their chances of discovering themselves as effective moral educators?

These tensions are creative, just as the tensions between theory and practice are creative, because they can lead to a vision of what it is we ought to be doing as educators. This book offers a modest beginning toward that goal.

The book tells three stories. The first and most obvious one is what happened at Exeter's first Bicentennial Summer Institute. To help tell that story I have selected passages from a journal kept by a participant in the Institute, L. Timothy Doty, formerly of Hotchkiss, now of Ravenscroft School in Raleigh. Think of the passages from his journal which I have intertwined with the talks, the summaries of presentations and the reactions of observers as little interchapters catching the ambience of the Institute.

The Institute was deliberately designed to be an inductive process: we participants wanted to define our problems as we saw them and to reflect upon those problems before we asked our resource colleagues to come in and help us with them. Every one of our resource colleagues remarked on the freshness of this approach and were gratified to be a part of it.

The second story is of two leaders — Theodore R. Sizer and Stephen G. Kurtz. When Exeter invited Mr. Sizer to give the keynote address to the Institute, it was no perfunctory gesture to the other academy founded by a Phillips; Mr. Sizer's scholarship in, and long thinking about, moral education made him the obvious choice. He gave us a beginning.

Mr. Kurtz gave us an ending when he spoke at the concluding plenary session of the Institute, and the eloquence of his words attests to the seriousness of his commitment to John Phillips' charge.

In the argot of moral educators, Mr. Sizer represents the "contextual" approach to moral education, Mr. Kurtz the "didactic." Like all generalizations, that one denies full justice to the breadth of both men's visions, but it does suggest something of the difference in their approaches and of the mark they have put on their schools.

The third story is of what has happened at Exeter in moral education since the Institute, and if this story seems to have only modest achievements, it is through no lack of commitment, energy and imagination on the part of Harvard Knowles, David Weber and Stephen Kurtz. These men know that while great institutions like Phillips Exeter Academy are capable of self-examination, they are, nevertheless, slow to change. The pursuit of excellence at Exeter has traditionally meant academic excellence. The challenge is to persuade a distinguished faculty that the pursuit of moral excellence will not compromise intellectual distinction; it will, in fact, enhance it.

I have chosen to write a Prologue and Epilogue rather than a conventional Introduction and Conclusion because I do not want the reader to assume that there are neat summary statements available for this complex subject, even though Thomas Holcombe's talk and Charles Twichell's report — both in the Appendix — could serve, the first as an introduction to important problems of moral education, the second as a conclusion providing some solutions. I have included my talk at Andover in March, 1979, and my essay "Moral Education," written for Exeter's Bicentennial book on teaching, but I know that in those papers I have revealed only one point of vantage for examining the subject. My colleagues in this endeavor represent other perspectives, and the stimulation of this book will come from the reader's sense of a unity made all the richer by a diversity of attitudes. The reader should join the process of reflection herein and strive to make his own synthesis of ideas.

My wife has listened to my prose and my ideas for this book for many hours, and she has always encouraged me to press on in my hope to honor the founder of Exeter. Edith Leonard Greene has not only typed the entire text, she has also done it cheerfully, always discovering the right words of encouragement at every stage of my work. And my friend and colleague Paul Sadler, Jr., Editor of The Phillips Exeter Academy Press, has been a patient teacher.

Charles L. Terry

Exeter, 1981

I

PROLOGUE

That Phillips Exeter Academy should have chosen moral education as the subject for its first Bicentennial Summer Institute is not surprising. In addition to John Phillips' famous charge, there is more current urgency: there is the report of the Evaluation Committee of the New England Association of Schools and Colleges in the fall of 1976 which observed at Exeter "a strong tendency for some faculty [members] to assume that knowledge and goodness were almost completely interchangeable concepts and to restate any question about 'goodness' as though it were a question about 'knowledge.'" They went on to observe: "It is perhaps worth noting that many students and even some faculty [members] have the same perception, namely that the quest for academic excellence sometimes crowds out the quest for moral excellence." And, finally, there is the personal and professional character of Stephen Kurtz, the Principal. It was his decision to pursue the subject for Exeter's first Bicentennial Summer Institute.

Accordingly, we set about writing a proposal to be submitted to foundations: "Can Our Schools Teach Personal Morality?" We were most fortunate to get the generous help of the Esther A. and Joseph Klingenstein Fund and the DeWitt Wallace Fund to support an institute at Exeter; and in the fall of 1977 four Exeter faculty members met in Cambridge, Massachusetts, with Lawrence Kohlberg, Director of the Center for Moral Education at Harvard, Theodore R. Sizer, Headmaster of Phillips Academy, Andover, David Mallery of The National Association of Independent Schools and Christopher Brookfield, Dean of the Church Schools of Virginia. These advisers gave us many wise suggestions, but chiefly, that we should limit our participants to those from faculties in private boarding schools like Exeter because in doing so we could achieve a manageable focus on the subject and its problems. Therefore, we invited six schools — Andover, Choate-Rosemary Hall, Deerfield, Hotchkiss, Lawrenceville and St. Paul's — schools whose faculties and staffs have long enjoyed informal contact with one another.

In the spring of 1978 the directors of the forthcoming Summer Institute on Moral Education held a planning meeting at Exeter attended by a representative from each of the seven participating schools. Mindful of the advice of our Cambridge consultants that we give the participants a share in planning the Institute's proceedings and intent upon establishing an investigation of the subject along inductive lines, namely, bringing in resource people after we had carefully considered our unique common problems, we set about defining the goals for the Institute. We agreed to concentrate on these goals: the clarification for each participant of his or her own role as a moral educator; an evaluation of the ethos of each of our schools; and a program for effecting worthwhile reflection on moral education at each of our schools.

Thanks to Mr. Sizer's background and talents — a former dean of the Harvard Graduate School of Education and a present principal instructor at Andover — we had the rare opportunity of being introduced to our study theoretically and practically. However, Mr. Sizer's excellent address at the opening of the Institute was in the spirit of our intention to be inductive, to brood creatively on our own common problems; from the beginning of our thinking about the subject he had urged us to look at our own institutions which are so similar, to see what enormous opportunities lie close at hand in boarding schools charged with the imperative to nurture the character of our students. "We ought to take a look at our own total environments as the most promising way of pursuing moral education. If one seriously questions the direct approach, or the didactic approach, and I think one has to if one's honest and looks at the evidence, then one turns to the contextual approach primarily. One has to look at our institutions whole, in all our aspects."

We took Sizer's advice and the kinds of examinations we pursued proved to be most fruitful. We did not ask questions about how we might devise new courses for our curricula so that we could "teach goodness" more effectively; we looked at the nature and quality of our living in boarding schools and especially at our difficulties in communicating our concerns to colleagues who might be skeptical of or even, perhaps, hostile to, directing time, energy and serious commitment to those elements of our corporate lives not traditionally thought to be productive of academic excellence. We often talked about the need to confront colleagues on our differences with them in respect to the ethos of the school.

Concerned as we were with our forthcoming task of taking what we had been thinking back to our colleagues, we were often deliberating on the rhetoric and politics of effecting change. And we asked our principal resource colleagues, Lawrence Kohlberg and Douglas Heath, how we could get their help in devising good strategies for such change. They were most helpful in this request; they have wide experience in dealing with the politics of schools. But they urged us to consider other vital matters, too.

Kohlberg, though he has become more interested in the contextual approach to moral education than he formerly was, did make a plea for dignifying the study of ethics and especially for getting students to think about universal values. Heath observed that our approach, so devoted as it had been to the total context of boarding schools, had neglected the enormously important context of the classroom.

When the Institute ended, some participants stated that they looked forward most to going back to their classrooms and trying out some of the ideas Kohlberg and Heath had suggested. One might construe this intention as an evasion of the more formidable task of confronting colleagues unwilling to be reflective about the moral atmosphere of their schools. However, it was probably a result of our two weeks' saturation in contextual approaches and our growing awareness that didactic approaches, no matter how limited they might seem, are imperative in a society finding "values clarification" appealing. Such exercises do not allow teachers to declare what they believe. Mr. Kurtz's talk, coming at the end of the Institute, provided the model for powerful didactic roles that give expression to a teacher's beliefs.

So there is a progression in this book from contextual to didactic orientations, but such a progression does not establish the comparative value of one over the other, for they are best held in a tension, counterbalancing each other, of necessity, complementary.

II

MORAL EDUCATION: PROVOCATIONS FOR AN INSTITUTE*

Theodore R. Sizer

A concern for "moral education" is not an optional burden for either of the Phillips Academies. Andover's 1778 *Constitution* — which is mirrored by Exeter's, written three years later — is explicit on the matter:

> But above all, it is expected that the attention of instructors to the disposition of the minds and morals of the youth under their charge will *exceed every other care;* well considering that though goodness without knowledge is weak and feeble, yet knowledge without goodness is dangerous, and that both united form the noblest character; and lay the surest foundation of usefulness to mankind.

This charge runs like a red line through the entire document. Of course many other independent schools, particularly those that rest on church foundations, have similar strictures (albeit not as boldly stated), and most of us in 1980 in our catalogues articulate our schools' responsibility for "moral" as well as academic development. We talk of rules (which have the primary task of control on the community, but are not in fact necessarily very good teachers) and of "chapel services" and their like (which are at best inefficient provocations for moral conduct). But we rarely bother to define our terms or carefully outline how moral growth might take place on our campuses. It is at this *lacuna* that this conference is directed.

---

*Adapted from remarks made at the Phillips Exeter Academy Institute on Moral Education, June 1978.

Moral Education. A good and useable definition of both words is needed. Lawrence Cremin in his recently published John Dewey essays entitled *Public Education* makes the obvious point that "in the ordinary course of living education is incidental," that we are learning more or less all the time. Any interaction — in the cafeteria, in the supermarket, at the dinner table — is potentially educative; we are often and profoundly affected by the content of such usually serendipitous experiences. By contrast, schooling is intentional: we organize predictable experience to affect a student in desired ways. Schooling is deliberately planned; as Cremin says:

> I have found it fruitful to define education as the deliberate, systematic and sustained effort to transmit, invoke or acquire knowledge, attitudes, values, skills or sensibilities as well as any outcomes of that effort.

The key is deliberate intention, the experience for learning by someone (the student) planned by someone else (the teacher). This definition of education-as-deliberate-schooling is obviously narrower than "socialization," and puts "incidental" learning, which is always going on, in minor key.

There are two kinds of "deliberate education," didactic and contextual. The didactic mode is direct teaching, usually in the form of structured classes or meetings. The contextual is the learning that emerges from a deliberately designed environment, and the intentional, but implicit, educational messages emanating from it. Both are important.

So much for the latter of the two words. What of "moral"? There are a plethora of meanings from which to draw. For our purposes, three need review. For some concerned with moral education in schools, "moral" is an adjective applied to specific activities: these acts are either "good" (moral) or "bad" (immoral). Stealing is immoral (bad); telling the truth is moral (good). For others, it is used to denote vehicles that lead to actions, situational arrangements which can (more or less) lead to "good" or "bad" decisions by students. A "moral" vehicle, for example, could be a rule prohibiting gambling, serving as a device to encourage the learning of a "good" act, "non-gambling". For yet others, "moral" might refer to a process which when followed would lead to acts based on high principle (e.g., moral, "good" acts). This third definition, though difficult to articulate, is the most satisfactory. It posits that action taken after orderly reflection which is based upon principle (for example, "fairness" or "justice") is more likely to be "moral" (fair) than that which is impulsive, or unreflectively situational. A moral person, it is argued, acts on principle; to act on principle requires systematic reflection and a sense of the most desirable governing standard. Schools should teach how this systematic reflection takes place, what standards (such as justice or charity) might best apply as the basis for judgments, and why this conception of a moral life is worthwhile.

"Moral education," then, is the intentional process of developing through deliberate means a basis for a student's reflection and decision-making that results in his or her principled conduct. Note that moral education, for me at least, is not a list of rules, painted on the schoolhouse wall. Nor is it (as Lawrence Kohlberg would say) "a bag of virtues," a rigid list of "thou shalts..." and "thou shalt nots...." Nor does it rest on any theology or basis of faith; it is rooted in a tradition of rationalist, secular ethics.

Obviously, this construction of "moral education" begs a host of questions. Which standard is most appropriate to guide our actions, or are there a number of complementary standards? Surely any group of concerned persons will disagree on these matters — as well it should — but I suggest that the group of school people at this gathering at Exeter could quickly come to agreement on at least three key principles, or standards, which should be at the heart of our programs: fairness; compassion; and commitment to service. Furthermore, most of our colleagues, students and their parents, trustees and graduates would agree. And these three represent alone a major objective for moral education. Argument over additions to the list is less important at this juncture, in my opinion, than sorting out carefully what we mean, theoretically and practically, by each of these three concepts, and how these may be related to a process of reflection that leads, ultimately, to moral action.

Even as a teacher sharpens the definitions of these principles, there still remains the problem of application. How does one learn to be fair, compassionate and charitable? Clearly there are no clear "answers" to tell young people that apply in every situation: conditions vary in myriad ways. The process is the key; and how does one learn it — and teach it?

The most popular approach these days is the didactic, programs of "moral education" that involve direct, classroom instruction. Such is not surprising: most educators, when confronted by some social problem, conspire for its solution by creating a "course" about it. Most of us have used one or both of two approaches: classroom instruction which usually turns around case studies or "moral dilemmas" which are the basis for discussion; and school assemblies that depend either on hortatory disquisitions by school principals (such as myself) or by testimonials from significant figures who appear to be useful role models for the students.

The best known apostles of the former approach are Sidney B. Simon of the University of Massachusetts and Lawrence Kohlberg of Harvard. Simon's focus is on clarification; it rests on the assumption that if one accurately sees a situation in all its complexity, one will act "better" than if one merely blundered into decisions. Furthermore, a person who is used to clarifying ideas is unlikely to be the victim of indoctrination, a condition which limits freedom. Thus Simon's approach encourages students to pull issues apart, and in so doing learn a process of careful skepticism and evaluation, one which leads to ever clearer thinking about moral issues. Kohlberg's approach rests on several generations of research on moral development in humans, work initiated by Jean Piaget and pursued by Kohlberg himself over twenty years. Kohlberg has identified a series of stages of moral growth that appear (for males, at least) to hold up in a variety of cultures and traditions and across ages. One passes from the lower to higher levels, Kohlberg shows; however, few attain the highest "stage" of moral development, which is a life lived wholly on the basis of principle (and principle for Kohlberg rests on a particular conception of justice). For our purposes here, it is useful to report Kohlberg's argument that one can intentionally and deliberately provoke a student's movement from lower to higher levels through a formal, didactic process, largely through debate about moral dilemmas, which teach people, through their own experience in this process, the value of deciding upon issues in a principled — i.e., just — way. Simon's and Kohlberg's approaches have much in common, including their dependence on formal, didactic instruction, usually in the form of a structured class discussion built around a case study of a moral issue.

The approach of "preaching" has a long tradition, from Jonathan Edwards to Billy Graham. In spite of testimonials from old grads who report, often in their cups, that they learned all about what was good and what was sordid from old Dr. Sneezix in '33 at Evening Prayers, the record is hardly encouraging. Telling people what they should believe leaves much to chance; as each student is not deliberately engaged in sharpening the issues for himself or herself and feels no special obligation to be involved or even to listen, the "chapel talks" route tends to have a low yield. And if there is recognition that moral conduct is, ultimately, the result of autonomous decision, with all the subtle variations possible even around a commonly-held principle such as justice, the ability of a single speaker to tell very much except obvious generalities is limited.

"Preaching" is useful (in my experience, at any rate) only in setting an agenda, in clarifying some issue facing a community and in raising student's consciousnesses to some topic or another.

However, does clarification *per se* necessarily lead to principled conduct? If people say that they would do certain things in certain situations, will they in fact so act when those situations actually arise? The evidence is spotty — not surprisingly so, given the complexity of the issues to be weighed. One is made a bit skeptical, however, by the experience of Harvard's Donald W. Oliver, whose social studies curriculum on social issues, extensively developed and evaluated during the 1960's, was adjudged by him to have been a failure on a number of important counts. After discussing a series of this curriculum's "cases" — say, on the rights of labor and management — the involved students could articulate the key issues and could well sort out the principles involved. However, six months or more later, there was no evidence that they acted in any new way as a result of the program; indeed, the issues and principles themselves seemed to recede in the students' consciousness. A didactic approach, carried on in a single, separate class and relatively unconnected with the tone of the overall institution, seems to have limited impact. The "surround," the context provided by the institution itself, seems to be a powerful, if implicit, teacher.

There is some provocative evidence about the contextual basis for moral education, particularly from the work of two scholars, one a political scientist and the other a sociologist, both — confusing to say — with the same name, James S. Coleman. The political scientist Coleman's work on colonial Nigeria outlines how a Westernized but African elite was developed, often in boarding schools, one which broke in a single generation from many tribal customs to an acceptance (for good or ill) of the virtue of European ambition and approaches to modernization. The schools which were the engine of this rapid, abrupt process were "total" communities; in their implicit and explicit regimens they consistently forwarded a set of Western values. Clearly they achieved their ends — so well that the graduates, schooled in the ways and attitudes of rights in a representative democracy, overthrew the colonial rulers and created an independent state. However, their post-Colonial polity was yet unabashedly Western in design and character: the values of Europe had taken surprising hold. And these values had been "taught" both didactically and contextually, with the context — the structured boarding school or university college — deliberately designed and of demonstrable power. This power of "total communities" for political socialization has not been lost on other societies, including modern Cuba and the People's Republic of China.

The sociologist Coleman is best known for the federally-sponsored and funded survey of equal educational opportunity completed in the late '60's of which he was Director and which, in the shorthand of such efforts, is usually referred to as "the Coleman Report." The study provided correlations among a wide variety of factors in elementary and secondary school children's formal education and wider lives, including the factor of race. Some 640,000 children were included, making the survey one of the most sweeping in American experience. The data suggest many conclusions, some supportive of the conventional wisdom, some not. For example, the social class of a student (defined in terms of parental income) appears to correlate far more closely with academic achievement than does racial identification. Poor youngsters appeared to learn less (defined in terms of achievement tests in academic subjects) than did wealthier children — except in schools in which the poor children represented a minority of 40% or less. One can readily hypothesize that the "tone" of such schools would be dominated by wealthier students, who characteristically are more accepting of the diligent about the goals set by teachers. The context, then — the subtle tone of the school, the mix of attitudes and aspirations of peers — "taught." The lesson for moral education is obvious.

If one compares the power of "context" with that of the "didactic" method, one is quickly reminded that many of Kohlberg's most significant positive findings about the effectiveness of his moral discussions approach emerge from his work in Connecticut prisons. The context there — a community of people who shared a wish to get out — must have been powerful, and affecting the quality of the didactic sessions. It is no surprise that Kohlberg's recent work — such as in the Cambridge (Massachusetts) "Cluster School" — has included efforts at creating intentional "just communities" — principled contexts, as it were. Undoubtedly context is important, indeed crucial.

What are my conclusions, to serve as provocations for this conference? Focus first and primarily on *contextual* concerns, as these provide the most promising route for moral education. The schools represented at this conference are boarding schools: reflect on the lessons which Coleman relates about Nigeria.

Test our existing schools against the key principles of justice, charity and service. Are they consistently "fair"? Are they compassionate? Do they provoke a selfless commitment to service (and not an arrogant *noblesse oblige* attitude long associated with schools of our sort)? Do we show respect of and for our students; do we treat them with dignity? (Too often not, I fear: the very notion of considering a fourteen-year-old to have dignity is lamentably foreign in some quarters.) Do we watch for hypocrisy in our conduct — joking at one moment about last Saturday's faculty cocktail bash and at another hectoring as a sinner the furtive seventeen-year-old beer drinker? How sensitive — compassionate — are we, for example with dress codes, that silly symbol of correct behavior? Clothes are class uniforms: do we respect the feelings of students for whom striped ties and blazers are foreign? Do we recognize values that arise from class traditions (rather than matters of fundamental justice) and curb them? (No: I guess that these Northeastern "prep" schools are often mindlessly, and in fact cruelly, insensitive to class differences.) And finally, and most painfully, on justice: do we as well-endowed schools and recognized "charities" take special pains to focus our resources exclusively on the needy, or do we use our "charitable" resources to support the educational activities of the wealthy? It is difficult to teach justice in institutions that are insensitive to issues of justice on their own doorsteps. This is hard saying — but essential for schools such as ours to hear, to understand and to act upon. Hypocrisy is the adult trait held in most contempt by adolescents. Our institutions cannot purport to teach the values of fairness if they harbor, recognized or unrecognized, institutional injustice.

In a word, if we are interested in the moral education of our students, we must start with a searching look at the moral order of our own schools, of our own adult community and values. If the context is right, if we intentionally and deliberately create just and compassionate schools, their products are more likely to be just and compassionate than through any other pedagogy we might employ. Such is the power of a boarding school.

The path to moral education starts with us, not the students. Let us begin again at this conference by looking in the mirror.

Good luck—

Some Related Readings

Lawrence A. Cremin, *Public Education* (New York, 1976)

James S. Coleman, *Nigeria: Background to Nationalism* (Berkeley, 1960)

────── (ed.) *Education and Political Development* (Princeton, 1965)

James S. Coleman et al. *Equality of Educational Opportunity* (Washington, 1966)

David Purpel and Kevin Ryan (eds.) *Moral Education: It Comes With the Territory* (Berkeley, 1970)
— includes essays by Sidney Simon and Donald W. Oliver

Nancy F. Sizer and Theodore R. Sizer (eds.) *Moral Education: Five Lectures* (Cambridge, 1972)
— includes a chapter by Lawrence Kohlberg

From the Journal of Timothy Doty
June 19, 1978

The first day was spent making the initial presentations of the moral climate at the participants' respective schools, supposedly based on taped interviews with students. This turned out to be largely personal statements of problems and expectations by participants. Some interesting things came out: important relations among faculty; teachers as moral models; dissatisfaction of people with what they are conveying to the kids morally and feelings of impotence and frustration about prospects of doing much better. Also, one person expressed concern about what high-powered academic emphasis teaches in terms of aggressiveness, competitiveness, interest in personal achievement. But what should we emphasize? Meekness? Cooperativeness in intellectual endeavor? Sameness of effort and achievement?

One thing I am afraid of is that the Institute might not focus enough and try to solve or discuss too many problems which may be simply school problems, not specifically problems of moral education.

Small groups met in afternoon to discuss four questions. I don't think any of them discussed them systematically — certainly ours didn't. It was really more of a get-acquainted, what-do-you-think session. More of that tomorrow morning. Rules tend to dominate discussion, even when people don't want them to. People like to say that the rules don't involve morality, but I am not too sure of that. Moral problems arise if not in violations themselves, then in justice of responses to infractions. This also came out in some of the interviews which were played or described.

III

SUMMARY OF THE FIRST PLENARY SESSION

On the first full day of the Institute we heard presentations from each school — the basic issue addressed, What is the moral atmosphere of your institution? The participants had been asked to interview students on their campuses to help them assess moral education at their schools. The presentations covered a wide range of observations and opinions, and on occasion participants would remark on the differences, some apparently striking, between one school and the others; nevertheless, a distinct cluster of common problems and preoccupations emerged. It was clear that we had been well-advised to limit the participation in the Institute to independent boarding schools.

Almost from the moment of our beginning that opening day we discovered that a teacher's life is a busy and a lonely one: we too infrequently have time to reflect upon our professional lives and to exchange ideas with our colleagues. We found ourselves establishing a unique rapport with each other; we did not perceive ourselves as deans or as teachers of mathematics: we were people who had committed our professional lives to nurturing the young in schools, and we knew that we needed to reflect deeply on how to do that better than we had been doing it.

COMMUNITY

Naturally, we had much to say about our sense of community in a boarding school. We observed, for example, that there was a fair amount of diversity not only among the student population but among the faculty as well. This diversity in the faculty makes for a pluralistic moral world, probably rich in opportunity for moral development, but frustrating in the kind of confusion attendant upon such pluralism. Many of us noted a dilemma that grows out of such an atmosphere: we want our students to develop the kind of integrity enabling them to make moral choices, to become autonomous moral agents; but we also want standards, we want to agree on some basic premises of our community. One participant, incidentally, offered a distinction between these two desiderata: ethics as developing personal autonomy; morality as imposing standards externally. This is a useful distinction, one that complements the contextual versus the didactic approach to moral education.

A participant spoke about the "tone" that gets set when we thoughtlessly litter the campus or undo the work often lovingly done by the grounds crew; another spoke of the elitist, monied atmosphere of our campuses, sometimes in the midst of surrounding communities of scarcity. We noted the materialistic and extremely secular values that often breed such thoughtlessness and that seem to accompany the gossip-ridden, rumor-ridden ambience of a campus. We observed the negative egocentrism that projects discontent in such activity and vitiates the positive support that we felt used to exist in our communities. A participant noted that we seem to signal an alarming message to ourselves, and certainly to our students, in making the major privilege of seniority the release from obligations of responsibility within the community.

We seemed to be reaching a clear consensus about the nature of our communities: what is happening for the faculty is inevitably going to affect what is happening for the students. Several participants spoke at some length on the emotional and spiritual inhibitions of our faculties and noted that the values that almost invariably get articulated are intellectual ones. Our students want an atmosphere of affection, of caring, of unselfishness — of living for others — and yet we realized that this atmosphere cannot be achieved when faculty members are unwilling to risk humane intimacy with each other and with their students. We knew, that is, that understanding the way a faculty deals with itself is a prerequisite for establishing a program of moral education.

FACULTY

Two words constantly reappeared in our dicussions of the way a faculty deals with itself: we often spoke of the paucity of "confrontation" and of "reflection." We do not have the courage to confront our colleagues when we disagree with their actions or their principles, and we do not have the courage to reflect on the question "Excellence for what?" Too often "excellence" is a code term for our evasion of discussing the values that ought to inform our philosophy of education. We are altogether too busy, too compulsive with each other and too willing to let busyness and professional competition become the substitutes for the tradition that we feel we have lost as our schools become more and more secular. The quotidian issues of discipline get our attention, not the permanent major issues, such as, for example, how a faculty becomes sensitive to the defensiveness of young people separated from their families.

As the stereotypical "good schoolman" increasingly emerges as a rarer and rarer antique, it is difficult to know with the old certainty what kinds of models we should be for our students. And as one participant suggested, we ask young teachers to carry on the standards without the traditions once available in our schools. Individual teachers in our schools are uncertain about their roles in the community.

STUDENTS

This faculty uncertainty about itself is compounded by its uncertainty about students' values. "I understand what the students are saying," noted one participant, "but I don't understand *why* they're saying it." The uncertainty often makes our response to student misbehavior confusing: in the extreme we oversentimentalize compassion or we overlegalize fairness.

But about some matters central to students' experience we appear to be more certain. For example, we often noted the formidable power of "peer pressure," so omnipresent a reality despite the hackneyed sound of the cliché. The "peer pressure" is so strong that it overpowers our attempts to make restraint a virtue, to exhort students to find the beginnings of self-discipline in conforming to the rules. Students frequently complain not only of a high degree of competition but of an ugly cliquishness in their community, and these aspects of life of course exacerbate the pressures of the group. We often noted the critical absence of "support systems" for the young student separated from his parents, and one participant observed that perhaps the students' morals are fairly well set when they arrive at our schools, but that their behavior is not, and that these conditions make for the vulnerability of the student to "peer pressure."

Students face a sense of loss, of deracination, and because of this sense and their perception that "the rules" are the faculty's morality, they rebel in anger. Much of the vandalism and partying, we felt, is attributable to such anger. Students realize that a community cannot function properly when there are no prohibitions on hedonism, but they do not consider such prohibitions "moral," rather they are "practical." And so student attitudes are schizophrenic: angry that a faculty is so trivial as to mistake "rules" for morals, and yet willing to admit that the community cannot function without restraints; resenting the imposition of values upon them, yet eager to be in an environment that fosters moral growth.

Students must be enabled to realize, one participant stated, that acts have consequences, even not getting caught has consequences. But in our ruthless pursuit of academic excellence we breed a selfishness and a destructive competitiveness that blind our students to the truism — acts have consequences.

We want to bring out the best in them so we challenge them to be "excellent"; but often the effect of our challenge is to debilitate them morally. They, for their part, want an affectionate and humane community; but often their behavior is arrogant and often it is apathetic.

ADMINISTRATION

As we speculated on the roots of our troubles — an absence of tradition, a compulsive routine causing overwork and at best superficial attention to questions of value — we became aware of the urgent need for administrative leadership if we hoped to do anything about moral education. Those in positions of leadership must, we noted, build a spirit of colleagueship in our faculties so that we can be open with each other and reflective about what it is we are really trying to do. "Excellence" for what?

June 20

Small groups met again this morning. I think we are coming to understand each other more now, though it is still difficult to cut through some of the rhetoric. We were getting specific ideas from some people in the evening session, especially from Tom Quirk of St. Paul's. Much of the emphasis seems to be focusing on inter-faculty relations. Steve and Blanche both seem taken with this idea — more willingness to speak to colleagues about personal or professional problems. I find that very difficult. My tendency is still to rely on the academic approach — if you teach people to think rigorously and clearly about ethics and moral decision-making — and that means giving them certain intellectual tools — then their thinking will affect their behavior.

I have felt tired most of the day. Slept all afternoon. That hasn't helped my participation in today's meetings.

Writing tomorrow.

June 22

Yesterday was spent writing. Steve and I produced statements to the faculty on the need for self-awareness in moral education. I think they are similar enough that we should be able to come to some kind of common statement, if we decide that is desirable. Blanche wrote more for her discussion group. I haven't read it yet.

Today Chris Brookfield and Dave Weber read responses to the meetings so far. Both were very good. Not much discussion following those presentations this morning.

In afternoon meetings, in two groups, more discussion. Things stayed pretty general and amorphous. When Brookfield tried to define as "religious" the entire intellectual or academic enterprise, I finally got exercised enough to speak up. Seems to me that we are in danger of defining "religion" or "morality" so broadly that they will lose all meaning. We need to decide, or at least to argue about, what morality really is, as well as what it is not. Only when that is clear will we have any luck deciding how to teach it, whether didactically or contextually or what.

Joe Reimer from the Harvard Graduate School of Education ended the session with a short talk. Talked about identifying the "culture" at a school which brings about certain kinds of behavior. I wasn't too clear on that, but it sounded good. He did recommend a book on the subject. Also exhorted us to be very clear about what we mean by "moral," etc., very concrete. Music to my ears.

IV

OBSERVATIONS ON THREE DAYS OF THE INSTITUTE

DAVID R. WEBER

Most of what Chris and I have to say is either descriptions as we try to summarize and focus things that have been said in the past three or four days or else argumentative reactions to directions that the Institute has been taking. I wanted to begin with two observations of a different kind.

I've been struck from Monday on by how wide the differences are in the agendas that different people have brought with them to the Institute. I think there's some divergence of view about the nature of the change that should take place in our schools, and I know that there's an extreme divergence of views about the degree of change that is needed. The great thing is that people have been willing, and are willing, not to give up but to suspend the pursuit of their own goals to help others in the group make progress in pursuing their own goals. There's a spirit of collegiality and cooperation, and Chris and I hope the same spirit will prevail today since it's been impossible for us to give equal weight to all the ideas and issues that have been raised. Some of you will hear us emphasize concerns that are closer to your own concerns than others will. The spirit that says if it's on your agenda, it's on my agenda is a very nice spirit, and one that seems particularly appropriate and fortunate in a group concerned about moral education.

Second, I've been more and more struck by the intensity of the ambivalence that many people here feel about the change that we're trying to move toward. On the one hand, it is intensely desired, it is seen as critical to the lives that we lead now and to the lives of our students. On the other hand, there is enormous anxiety about the difficulties attached to achieving this change once we are back at our own schools. Anxiety about how hard it will be to do it, and even how risky it will be to try to bring it about. I hope that in the small groups or elsewhere, perhaps in the school teams, this anxiety will be faced squarely and that strategies that are emerging will take it into account.

CHRISTOPHER M. BROOKFIELD

I was enjoined to give careful attention to what it is that I've been hearing in the groups, in your presentations, in our conversations, even, I suppose, at the cocktails. So this is a brief response to that, and I guess the question that I'm asking is, "What do I hear from the briar patch of our anxiety and ignorance four days along the thorny path of moral education?" More cries for help than cries of outrage, more caring than self concern, more courageous questions than cryptic copouts. I hear a lot of talk about competition and peer pressure, about lack of time and lack of love in our various communities. All of you articulate those concerns. A great many people are perplexed about the problems of pot and rule-breaking, about the agonies of life inside the dormitory and the emptiness of life outside the classroom, about modes of modeling and the importance of hiring teachers who are willing to be appropriate role models. Much to our dismay, perhaps, it has become clear that our common problems point to our common humanity and inhumanities rather than to the impossibility of exchange on account of our impossible uniqueness.

We seem to accept as a worthy goal Vince Avery's emphasis on the education of our students and faculty in principled thinking. We are less willing to agree with Ted Sizer's suggestion that justice, compassion, and commitment to service can comprise a sufficient set of common principles underlying moral education. Some of us can agree with Sam Harding and John Anderson that one of the aims of a program in moral education should be to allow students to accept, understand, explore and confront themselves — on the theory that a community which extends trust and generosity leads persons to affirm their dignity and self-worth and extend the same options toward others. Some of us are uneasy about possible problems suggested by the proposition that examining the way the faculty deals with itself is a prerequisite for addressing the way students deal with the community.

One question that we appear reluctant to explore in any rigorous way thus far is Alden Flanders' query, "Do we want agreement on standards and behavior in our schools or do we want mature individuals with integrity who can make their own decisions?" We have not as yet made our peace with Harvey Knowles' question, "Should we not explore the ways in which the environment of the boarding school is the repository of moral values rather than try to devise a special academic curriculum that will inculcate them." (I take it that we have all bought Ted Sizer's conviction that because of its 24-hour-a-day curriculum, the boarding school is particularly well suited to a program of moral education.) Tim Doty has made the sagacious plea that we not allow the definition of moral education to get so broad that we are reduced to discussing issues of school life only.

DAVID R. WEBER

I've tried to approach the same question in the manner of abstracting themes or trying to define areas of concern which might become more limited subjects or topics for small groups.

So what I want to refer to now is a description of four different areas of concern that seem to me to dominate other areas of concern in the Institute so far — perhaps with an eye to having a group choose one of these as a specific area to go after in a more pragmatic way.

The first concern, to borrow Ted Sizer's vocabulary, is changing the "surround," the moral environment provided by the school, since at the moment we have grave reservations about what our students are learning besides their skills, grave reservations about what values our institutions are actually reinforcing in our students' experience. We would like to find ways to let our students feel more consistently than they do that they are respected as individuals and that the school aspires to more for them than competence, excellence, achievement and success. We do not see ourselves, and we do not want our students to see our schools, as staging areas in the assault on the Admissions Committees of prestigious colleges.

Second, we want to change the relationships which presently obtain in our faculties. Many of us feel isolated, we feel that we condescended to by colleagues who see us as soft, we feel powerless to change the behavior of colleagues who belittle or humiliate students, we feel frustrated, or even self-contemptuous, when we remain passive in the face of such behavior. It is not only students whose moral development or whose ability to live up to their own values is threatened by peer pressure.

Third, we need more clarity and consensus than we have about what values we hold in common and how to go about encouraging their growth in our students.

And fourth, we need to be more thoughtful about our rules and punishments: to have rules which reflect our values, and not have rules which contradict our values or our educational objectives. I remember on Monday one school saying we preach honesty and fire for it, we preach individuality and require conformity, we preach abstinence and wink at discreet indiscretions. We are frustrated by seeming to reward dishonesty and penalize honesty. We feel compromised by rules or punishments which violate our own values, or which at least make us feel silly and therefore demeaned in our roles as enforcers; we need either to persuade our students that our rules and penalties are just and fair, or to persuade ourselves, at least, of that so that we can comfortably defend the rules, believe in them, and contend for them in dealings with students.

CHRISTOPHER M. BROOKFIELD

Westerners, as Easterners will tell you, have short memories. With the possible exception of one highly publicized event in the history of Western Christendom, most of us have trouble remembering what happened in anything as long as a three-day period. Nevertheless, I should like to recall for you certain *bon mots* which still retain their enticing aroma amid all the verbiage we have served up to one another since the schools' presentations last Monday. Here are some of the enduring, if not endearing, flavors from those presentations which continue to make my moral education mouth water even after three days' entombment. (In alphabetical order, of course):

Vince Avery's intriguing question, "What would Andover die for?" should give even the sleekest of us trouble sleeping a night. Let the ghost of Avery stalk the Institute to the very end.

Charles Twichell's injunction that we keep ourselves "at the litter level" ought to inform any institutional reform we may choose to affirm.

We need to be needled by Parney Hagerman's deceptively simple solution to her own question, "What is morality? It's obviously different for all schools."

Chuck Hamblet's refrain is one that most of our schools have heard repeatedly but heeded only half-heartedly: "We must develop caring along with academic achievement." (As I have said elsewhere, compassion need not compromise excellence.)

Steve Bolmer's plea has probably been dew on the parched lips of countless of our colleagues, and we ought not to forget it after the Institute. Namely: "I understand what the kids are saying; I can't figure out why they're saying it."

Sam Harding's comment that certain aspects of a house system can promote divisiveness and defensiveness and exclude serious criticism is also applicable to Exeter's compartmental departmental system, and so on. . . .

Alden Flanders' concern, which Karl Roehrig echoes over and over in concomitant chorus, is crucial: "All acts have consequences. We must help our constituencies to become more sensitive to the consequences of what we do in our communities."

John Anderson's paraphrase ought to be perpetuated. "Give students the rules and they will be moral for a day. Teach them to make rules for themselves and they will be moral for the rest of their lives."

Nat Smith said, "We need to help one another to be courageous enough to go back to our schools and challenge where we didn't before."

Ellie Drury pleads, "We've got to make rules realistic enough so that we can enforce them."

Susan Jorgensen reminds us, "We need to address the way we deal with students and with each other."

Blanche Hoar points out that "Students want to have room to shape their own values at the same time that they want the faculty to have a strong sense of what they believe in." That tension might be worth holding.

One thing has become increasingly clear: we must become more sensitive to the complexities of the moral issues which involve both students and faculty.

DAVID R. WEBER

The next segment in this presentation is the longest one. I found myself very stimulated by Ted Sizer's keynote address on Sunday, and it's in the background of this piece, which is actually to a large extent in disagreement with some of what he said. This is a statement about what he calls "the surround, the context, the moral environment," and it falls into two parts. The first one is an approach to the problem; the second, an approach to a solution.

Students must sense, often unconsciously, that their schools stand for something, that the school's way of life affirms some values and lets others go. The reports from the schools on Monday were eloquent and emphatic about this: Many or all of our schools are unwittingly teaching the wrong things, at least some of the time. John said of Deerfield that to go there is to place oneself within an elitist and monied context when in the country and the world at large scarcity, poverty, deprivation are widespread. Because the risk of forgetting compassion is so large in such a surround, the school has Alternative Systems of Education, including internships in Roxbury and a program that places Deerfield students within the local farming community. These experiences have proven to be powerfully educational. What an irony, if the implications are as large as they seem: do the most prestigious secondary institutions in the country have to get their students off campus in order to educate them morally as well as intellectually? One participant said that the monosexual context has a powerful educational message — that girls, and by extension women, are distracting diversions, destined for separate, subordinate roles. If that is true, the implications are immense. It would take an awful lot of the didactic to offset a context that functioned in that way. Vince described Andover as a secular, capitalistic school dedicated to the ruthless, aggressive pursuit of excellence. All of us have known students who graduated from our schools with great academic distinction but with minimal interest in other people, with imperceptible commitments to compassion or service. All of us want to work in schools that *try* to nourish and that *tend* to nourish a different, less selfish, orientation toward life. Ted Sizer urged us on Sunday to see residential schools as especially obligated to create environments which would encourage principled decision-making, not sophisticated selfishness, in their students. The question, How can we do this? is perhaps the large question which arches over the rich and intimidating variety of the more specific issues that have been raised here in the past few days.

I would like to offer the hypothesis that a crucial aspect of this problem for most, if not all, of our schools is their secularity. A school that identifies itself with a religious tradition is likely to project a different sense of its deepest value commitments from one that has no explicit religious identification. I remember being very struck on Monday when Vince Avery said that there was an absence of tradition at Andover and Harvey Knowles said that at Exeter tradition is very powerful, that among other things it inhibits change. My guess is that they are both right — *about both schools,* and probably about other schools in our group. The Calvinist tradition that Steve Kurtz referred to on Sunday night as the founding impetus behind Exeter and Andover is dead — dead *as a set of religious ideas or values* centrally affirmed by the school, but it lives on (at Exeter, at least) in a secular form — in a solemn, severe institutional style, a comprehensively judgmental attitude that the student feels weighing on him. My point is that when the religious tradition is alive and visible, when it is a central part of the school's sense of itself, the "Calvinism" provides a moral context for the students' individual strivings; it can transmit itself to students as piety, as humility, as commitment to service; but that when the religious tradition is not alive and not visible the Calvinist residue is perceived by students to be merely autocratic, constricting, arbitrarily narrow.

How, since we are massively and visibly committed to the inculcation of academic skills, and since we no longer do have the visible presence of a powerful, shared religious tradition with its symbols and its rituals, how can we convince our students that some things matter more to us than the acquisition of skills, than entrance into a prestigious college, than intellectual autonomy, than personal achievement? We do have important resources for this task, and while some of them have been clarified in powerful and moving ways since Sunday, others have, I think, been obscured or implicitly minimized, and I'd like to say something about them. Many or all of them may be obvious, but I think there may be some value in an inventory.

For one thing, the "surround" cannot be accurately defined only in cultural or political terms: the moral environment inhabited by any particular student is made up in large measure by the sum of his personal relationships with the people he sees a lot of. In my own learning experience, in college, if I understand it correctly, I had one teacher who influenced me morally more than the entire remainder of the "surround"; he changed the questions I asked, changed my scale of values. I hope that participants in this Institute are not hearing so much about devising programs and about contexts that seem to dwarf individuals that they lose confidence in their own individual roles as moral educators. A student perceives his surround one piece — one person — at a time, as well as organically, holistically, whatever. I hope this Institute will say to everyone here: "Like the school, you yourself are a moral educator whether you want to be or not." It is better to be thoughtful about it. Whatever your sense of the level of support you receive in your school, there is a community out there that cares about what you are trying to do.

There is also a level of action between the institution and the individual. One student attends a school that rarely meets as a school; that has no counselor; that offers or at least requires no course in ethics; whose administration and faculty shy away from preaching. Another is able to spend time talking with someone like Jef or Karl, spends at least a semester facing in a sustained way the moral dimensions of personal choices in a course framework, and lives at a school where the headmaster and, say, ten teachers speak publicly from time to time about moral issues of personal concern to them — not in a spirit of handing down the moral law but in the spirit of saying what they see and believe. I thought that one of the striking things about the Deerfield tapes was the students' readiness to see the faculty as models. The students don't want us to be moral autocrats — certainly Ted Sizer was right about the way in which efforts at "preaching" can backfire; but the students do want us to be moral advocates of a sort. Whether they agree with what we say is less likely to matter than their belief that we speak voluntarily and sincerely.

CHRISTOPHER M. BROOKFIELD

Recently I read an article commenting on Lawrence Kohlberg's theories. The burden of that article was to try to find a way to baptize the insights of Kohlberg on moral education in the current crusade for Christian education. (Why? Because once again, as in the time prior to the First World War, there is a demand for moral education in the classroom and Christian educators do not want to see the Bible take a back seat to the rostrum of developmental psychology.) One of the problems of such an alliance, holy or otherwise, is that, as the article puts it, "Kohlberg is trying to separate moral teaching from religion. He thinks that if he can show scientifically what moral development is, apart from religion, he will have an acceptable base for bringing moral teaching into the schools." The writer rightly makes clear various distinctions among advocates of moral education, values clarification, character education (the "bag of virtues" approach), and the like. Which brings me to the question of where I stand in the controversy.

The place whereon I choose to stand may not be one which is likely to move the earth. The only advantage of being antediluvian is that what was once venerable will more than likely become viable once again sometime before the next ice age. Two propositions to which I am unalterably attached are, first: that there is no such thing as values-free education or morally neutral instruction. In so far as the emperor in "The Emperor's Clothes" understood himself to be attired in royal finery, he was — but almost everyone else was unavoidably illumined by the bare facts. The fact is that there is no education which does not impart values or promulgate a faith (whether what is taught is no more exalted than the conviction that man is the measure of all things). For me, the question is not whether education ought to cast out the demons of indoctrination. The question is, What form of indoctrination is worthy of putting our faith in the educational process.

For example, as I have said elsewhere, a school's curriculum assumes more than its unstated understanding of how a person learns (an epistemology); since it unavoidably imparts judgment on what is worth learning, it thereby presupposes a theology as well: "Any assumption we make about the learning process and what is worth knowing also assumes a view of the nature of man and existence. At that point, it seems to me, theology — used in its broadest sense — becomes inseparable from epistemology, and religion and education are irrevocably interrelated." *(The Andover Review,* Spring 1977, p.36) Or, put another way, "If religion deals with the questions of meaning, purpose and value that we dare to raise with one another, then... the most profound questions that we hope education will engage us in are essentially religious." *(Andover Review,* p. 41)

The second proposition to which I am wedded is expressed in a phrase of one of my predecessors, which though it is not new is nonetheless true — namely: "Belief, not knowledge, determines action." No matter how much nor what kind of knowledge a student may have, it is what he believes that determines how his knowledge will be used. Or, to put it the other way around: How we act, what we choose to put our knowledge in the service of, is dependent upon what we have put out faith in. If that is true, then it seems clear to me that schools cannot avoid being concerned with religion in education because the goal of the educational process so defined is inescapably religious, regardless of what we may choose to label the various components of the curriculum in our school.

DAVID R. WEBER

On Sunday Ted Sizer proposed two agreements that would simplify and facilitate the work of this Institute. The first was that we accept the values of fairness, compassion, and a commitment to service as the principles we wanted to instill in our students; the second was that it would be more pertinent to talk about contextual education — the dynamics of the community — than about didactic education, the content of our courses. It seems to me that about forty percent of the group has bought the first agreement, the list — there has been a good deal of restlessness with that way of defining what we are trying to do. The group has so far bought the second agreement almost entirely. I'd like to propose a couple of revisions of the Sizer viewpoint.

As I think back on the experiences that seem to have produced whatever moral education has taken place in me, personally, I think of three: two were contextual, one didactic. First was my mother's continual demonstration — her modeling — of compassion; she gave me my first gut sense of the immense reality of the pain and the joy of other people, my first gut sense that that reality deeply mattered and demanded my respect and my loyalty. Second was the faith — it's the only possible word, since there was very little evidence — of friends that I was a better or more promising person than I seemed to be. Their faith made me or makes me try to be on good days the person they think I am and that I hope I am and want to be. Third was a course — not, as it happened, one in ethics but one in psychology. It explained the main defense mechanisms by which people try to make their own problems into someone else's problems; it helped me to catch myself when I start to do that, and it helped me deal with unfairness or hostility or anger in others, helped me to see or to guess where their aggression was coming from. So here are the revisions of Sizer:

1. It is a mistake to ignore the curriculum as a potential agent for moral education. Professor Oliver's evidence about the disappearance of effects after six months is interesting, but not to my mind decisive; my own experience contradicts it. Beyond that I think that students at schools as academically oriented as ours will continue to find it difficult to believe that we are serious about any enterprise that isn't reflected in some way in the formal curriculum. That's what they *know* we're serious about.
2. In defining how to try to bring moral education about, I find it less helpful to name a set of principles than to think about two processes — one in which we learn to see and feel the reality and the significance of others, and one in which we learn to understand the tendency in ourselves to play the ego's various games. When Ted had made his statement on Sunday, Karl said something like, "Ted, there isn't time in making most moral decisions to go through a list of principles and see what their applications are." There *is* time, though, to think about one's own motives. I am a lot more likely than I used to be to ask myself, when I feel myself getting defensive or angry, why I'm feeling that way. As a result, I am less likely to lay something on a student (or someone else) that belongs on me. I believe that there are ways of teaching these things to students, and that some of them can exist in a formal curriculum, and I hope that the Institute won't give up on the didactic altogether.

CHRISTOPHER M. BROOKFIELD

Having attempted to express what I feel is a positive response to where we have come so far, I have some questions and concerns about where things may be going. Some people have said somewhat nervously, "You mean we're supposed to develop something *con-*

crete to be implemented in the fall?" or "*I* am going to suggest a project to our faculty?" Such comments reflect an interesting philosophy of educational institutions if not a personal moral stance. It does seem odd that we can so easily despair of dealing with educational issues and retreat to the realm of "instruction" where, presumably, we know what we are doing. Having to come up with a specific program may even be more threatening than having to confront colleagues with it. When it comes down to the operation of the educational process, it seems only our students are free to fail. I would urge you to embrace the happy tension of risking failure rather than giving up the enterprise or, more likely, either talking it to death or coming up with what one of you has called "a bucket of scruples" incapable of being screwed into anything.

In this area I am fearful of what may become an easy out that Ted Sizer has offered us. You remember that he exhorted us to devote our efforts to the contextual rather than to the didactic because the carry over from classroom into life, as far as moral education is concerned, has "demonstrably low yield." Well, now, that is an interesting perspective for our schools which, without exception, protest that whatever else they do, what they are successful at, what they really are in business for, is what goes on in the classroom. Notwithstanding our failure in other human endeavors, are we so easily willing to give up the bag of tricks we have built our trade upon? One of you has voiced the hope that this Institute might become "a lodestar for education." If we arrive at the astounding insight that the classroom is after all irrelevant to any education for life, we may well start a revolution that will reshape independent education.

Perhaps somebody ought to begin asking the bizarre question of the relation of the classroom to the rest of the educational process in a 24-hour-a-day curriculum. Perhaps the "hidden curriculum" is what we teach most effectively at our institutions, but while we need to get a better grasp of what we are about there, we ought not to abandon the classroom which consumes at least a third of our waking day. However, any program in moral education has got to be part of our integrated curriculum rather than tacked on to it, and that poses some interesting problems for a great many of our schools whose curricula have probably been developed by the chicken coop method of accretion, shovel and patch — somehow inappropriate to what most of us regard as the castle of education we have erected. I hope that somehwere along the line you would embody the extravagant hope so aptly expressed by Parney Hagerman in her "Expectations" paper concerning this Institute. She said:

I would hope we could openly and honestly dissect our schools in terms of their "hidden curricula" to examine our disciplinary procedures, the classroom activities, the teaching techniques, the hiring/firing process, the messages of athletic contests, the activities in dormitories, in short, the entire operation of an educational institution.

Questions each school must seek to address concretely are: Where is moral education being taught in the total curriculum? Who is doing it? How? I take it that most of us have accepted that the "given" is not can we have a goodness curriculum (or whatever you want to call it) but what can we do with the one we've got? How can we redirect it in defensible ways? What should be its relation to any conscious program in moral education which we might see fit to develop?

V

MORAL EDUCATION AND THE CULTURE OF THE SCHOOL

Joseph Reimer

What usually happens when I come to give a talk is that I'm not at the school for more than five minutes before I have to speak. The first few minutes of my talk are devastating, at least for me, because I have just gotten off the plane, my head is still circling around the city, and I'm supposed to be talking about moral development. This is a wonderful idea, to allow me a generous time to acclimate myself. I have almost forgotten that I'm an observer here because in a short period of time I have become involved in the process that you're involved in. I can therefore speak with more involvement and passion than I usually do.

In speaking this afternoon about moral education I'm very close to what matters to me a great deal, and I have strong ideas on the subject. I also sense that this is a very responsive group; that's one of the nice things about being here. If some of the things I say make you want to put up your dukes, please do so, and I'll be glad to spar.

This morning when Chris and Dave were speaking, my first impression was, these are awfully big ideas. But then I began to hear a different agenda of small concrete problems: what to do about the girl who tells you about the terrorizing teacher, etc. Between "What Andover would die for," and how to deal with a terrorizing teacher there's a lot of space. It's into that space that I'd like to leap.

How to begin? Some ideas that I've jotted down: people generally agree that it would not be appropriate to go back in September waving the flag that we've been to Exeter and received the tablets from Sinai, and we are all now Moses come to bring you the law. Not much debate about that. On the other hand, some people thought that the best thing was to raise questions, to engage others in a process of inquiry, in a process of joint exploration and feeling such as the one that you are in fact going through now. It is in reaction to this second approach, which I see as being the more cogent of the two, that I'd like to respond this morning.

First, I'd like to recommend a book to you. It has been the most influential book I've read on educational change. It's by a professor at Yale, Seymour Sarason; the book is called *The Culture of the School and The Problem of Change.* [Boston: Allyn and Bacon, 1971.]

What Sarason does is to report on his observations of schools. He had written a major book on the anxieties of elementary school students learning to read and then realized that the problem wasn't in the classrooms, or even in the teachers, but in the culture of the school. That is, in that which is not purely individual, nor purely instructional, but in something more inclusive that could be called the culture of the school. He argues a school has a discernible culture that could be identified using an anthropological approach if one were patient enough to observe the behavioral and programmatic regularities that characterize the school. I want to talk about the culture of the school because I think it would be a helpful way to begin.

Sarason contends that reformers who attempt to initiate programmatic changes in the school's curriculum often fail because they are ignorant of the culture of the school. As an example he cites the establishment in the post-Sputnik era of a Master's program at Yale University for the training of secondary school teachers. At the urging of the university's president, the faculty agreed to establish this program designed to attract the highest caliber of college graduates and supply them more with courses in the subject matter they wanted to teach and less with the "how-to-teach-it" courses that usually comprise a training in education. But the students who entered the program were quickly disappointed, for they found that, on the one hand, many of the professors and graduate students who were in the graduate courses they took looked down upon them as "education majors" while, on the other hand, many of their students in high school could hardly understand, let alone care about, the intellectual nuances they were being trained by their courses to convey. The initiators of this program intended well by hoping to upgrade the training of secondary teachers, but by giving insufficient attention to the culture of the university (which as a graduate institution values most of the nuances of scholarly endeavor) and the culture of high schools (which has to educate a diverse group of adolescents whose curricular needs are highly varied), they created a nightmarish double-bind for the Master's candidates they were trying to help.

When Sarason talks about taking the culture into account in planning for curricular change, he is not simply referring to an exercise in blame — "who are the bad guys who will mess this up" — nor to an exercise in confrontation — "we know *you* are feeling hostile to this plan for change," but to an analysis of what features of the school environment are likely to pose problems for the implementation of the program and a construction of a realistic theory of change that will set out how and in what stages these problems will be dealt with. In the Yale example that would have meant a consideration of how a graduate seminar in, let's say, English literature would have structurally matched or mismatched the needs of a person training to teach English in an average high school. Since it would probably be unrealistic and unfair to expect graduate professors of English literature to restructure their courses to more fully meet the needs of this minority of students, consideration would need to be given to what alternative procedures (separate sections, tutorials, special courses) could be implemented, given the realities of budgetary and time constraints, to bridge the inevitable gap that would be created.

Turning to private secondary schools, if members of a faculty were concerned, as some of you are, with the problem of students getting cut down in class by their teachers, Sarason's approach would call for *not* attributing monstrosity to the teachers, not counting them out as beyond the pale, but asking about the context: what about the daily pressures that put the teacher in a situation where he or she is likely to act in such a way? And what is it in the culture of the school that we can change so that that teacher feels that these "reformers" aren't attacking me, but attacking the problem in its context.

Now that's a very involved and difficult task to achieve. You don't go right in and say I'm going to start with A, B, C, and D. You go in and say, What are the identifiable problems that I'm likely to have some success with in trying to change, that are likely to have some effect upon the problems that concern me. What can I discuss with other people that we can deal with together so that by looking at the problem in its context we're likely to come up with practical suggestions which will not run right up against the defenses of the people involved, but are likely to have import in changing what I call "the moral atmosphere" of the school?

This morning we spoke about establishing a "beachhead." I can't see how you could come to Exeter and quickly assess what is it about this place that makes it such that really good faculty people end up devouring boys and girls alive. Rather, it has to be a careful consideration of what are some specific situations in which boys and girls get eaten alive? What contributes to that happening? Maybe it is a single monstrous person. But more likely it is something in the way most teachers strive for intellectual excellence from their students that leads to a confrontation in which the slower students are put down for not keeping up with the standards. Since it is an enduring expectation that teachers will strive for excellence, the question is how can the striving be continued without having to lead to this problem in the class. David Weber's reference to the William Carlos Williams' story "The Use of Force" is pertinent here: there are ways the doctor can get the child to open her mouth.

You are going to meet Professor Kohlberg on Monday morning. He's going to have some very definite ideas about the nature of moral education. You have valued ambiguity; you have treasured a holding back of clarity, a coming together and an exploration of meaning. On Monday morning you're going to face the Professor; and he's going to come in with some very clear ideas. But it's just as well that you confront that challenge to be clear now because, as you were saying today, when you get back in September people are going to be much more direct in wanting to know what you mean by moral education. If you say — I'd like to help promote self-understanding among students, or to help students take responsibility — what do you mean by that? My sense from today is that you should go on valuing the tentativeness and many-sidedness, but also work toward much clearer, much more philosophic definitions of what you mean by these various concepts. Put them as principles that are dear to you, or a process that's dear to you, and try to spell out as extensively as you can exactly what you mean by those things. Throw them out to one another so that you can question one another. Often in trying to explain, let's say, what we mean by maturity, we use a tautology. "Oh, you know, maturity is acting maturely." Or we say it's learning to take responsibility without ever defining what we mean by responsibility.

When I think of defining responsibility — which for me is a central concept in adolescent moral education — I think of it not so much as a character trait as the way individuals organize their experiences in specific contexts. If we want students to act more responsibly, we have to consider in what context of the school we want them to so act. Educating for responsibility could be a sermon or it could be a message that could help someone understand something about herself in relation to others. If responsibility is defined as doing one's homework more regularly, it doesn't boil down to a rule — "do thy homework." Rather, in relation to a specific context doing one's homework can be agreed upon between student and teacher as the responsible thing to do. In another context they could both agree that only doing one's homework is not being responsible, and responsibility entails reading books outside the course because the course is too easy for the student and she needs to be responsible to do extra work to expand her mind. Contextual flexibility is extremely important, especially when dealing with extra-curricular activities.

To spell out in more detail what I mean by educating for responsibility, allow me to tell you about an incident which occurred in an alternative school I have been observing in the Boston area. One of its constant problems is use of drugs — marijuana — during extra-curricular school activities. Before a school trip, for example, the staff will devote a lot of time trying to reason with the students and have them come to an agreement about not using marijuana. An interesting process unfolds: students listen, agree and commit themselves to not using marijuana, and then on the trip they use it. When you ask them (as I do in interviews) "If you committed yourselves not to smoke marijuana, why did you smoke?" they say, "Don't you understand? I committed myself not to smoke marijuana in such a way that anyone else would get hurt." Or, "I said it would not be done so publicly that it would disrupt the order of the activity; but if I want to go off and smoke marijuana by myself where it will not disturb anyone else, that's not acting irresponsibly."

While their responses may exemplify what David Elkind has called "adolescent egocentricity," they can also teach us that a general pitch for student responsibility on the part of teachers and administrators can be simultaneously accepted and subverted by the students. They say, "Yes, I will be responsible," but mean by that something quite different from what the teachers intended. Until teachers learn to explicitly explore student meanings in relation to action-in-context (smoking marijuana alone in the woods), miscommunication, and perhaps miseducation, will continue.

To conclude my remarks, I would like to address the question of what you as teachers can realistically hope to achieve in returning to your schools next fall. I do not think that having been at the Institute will by itself suddenly give you new power to effect changes. But from my experience with moral education there are many things that teachers could do, whether it be in designing new courses or running student groups. There is one thing, though, that faculty members, at least individual faculty members, cannot do, and that is change the whole "surround." I agree with those people who said today it is a copout to rail against the mighty "surround." To decry the fact that achievement is an overriding value at Exeter or Andover or anywhere else seems to me to be playing Don Quixote. The objective is not to rail against achievement or competition or selfishness, but rather to begin within the realms in which you are responsible, in which you do have control. Begin by asking yourself how do you in your context bring other values and principles to play so that they can inform the existing, dominant values of achievement or competitiveness. Think about how mercy and justice can be merged together in the concrete here and now of your class, your dormitory.

In the schools I've worked with in the past years I have seen success in individual teachers introducing programs in moral education, defined in different ways, in a counseling, literature or religious program. Bringing moral education successfully to their school seemed to have required two things: the active backing of the administration and the teacher's faith that if he or she could succeed in his or her realm, others would hear about the success and become interested in incorporating this type of approach in their own classes. My sense is that if one can get administrative support and if one can develop a clear idea of what one would like to do in one's own area, and see how that fits into the larger culture of the school and has implications for the larger context of the school, then one can initiate the kind of "beachhead" model that has possibilities of working.

I've become extremely cautious in this field. I want to say to people it is a risky endeavor, the probability of success is not great. Before you buy into a program, before you go home and present yourselves to your colleagues, I think you ought to be clear as to what you want to do, clear about its justification, clear that you want to do this for students and not for your own self-glorification and clear about how this particular suggestion fits into the culture of the school. If you succeed, other people will turn to you and in their own way want to succeed in a way similar to yours. That doesn't mean coming in with the right answers or simply saying, "I came back from Exeter thinking moral education is a good thing which we ought to talk about." I don't see any possibility, in my limited experience, of succeeding in introducing change in a school if you are either too rigid or too vague. That is why I discussed the culture of the school and suggested a modest "beachhead" approach as a beginning step.

June 23

Morning session with Kegan and Reimer on developmental psychology. Kegan was very entertaining and very abstract — very much the young professor type. I found what he said stimulating, impressive, true, but I never could quite make the connection between what he was saying about kids' development and the way I work in the classroom. That gap really bothers me. Reimer came across with a sense of compassion and concern and understanding of kids and teaching. I would like to hear more from him.

The high point of the morning for everyone, I think, was Charles Twichell's description of his involvement in the Milgrim experiment.

Evening session was back in groups. We discussed discipline, counseling, differential treatment of 9th as opposed to 12th graders (or lower vs. upper schools). Then Sam Harding read his statement for Lawrenceville. Excellent. After that discussion I felt that many people were beginning to settle on real strategies when they return. These seem to focus on withdrawing ourselves from the forefront and bringing in outsiders to get the ball rolling. I think this is probably the best approach. None of this is going to last long if we try to go back and become residential experts on moral education. I'm afraid there is going to be a big run on Harvard School of Education talent this fall!

I do sense some positive movement now and I think it is the outsiders who are stimulating it.

VI

SUMMARY OF ROBERT KEGAN'S REMARKS

Robert Kegan addressed the Institute as a developmental psychologist, but the humanistic breadth of his vision enriched the specialty of his subject: "The natural curriculum" within all human beings, the "activity of meaning-making, of making sense of our experience." "One of the things at the heart of Piaget's vision," he noted, "is a kind of respect and intense curiosity about the meaning-making activity of children." He averred that one of the most powerful functions of education is addressing this activity and that moral education cannot effectively take place unless educators know something about "the meaning-making of our values."

Just as Lawrence Kohlberg would later claim that his theory of stages in moral development is "a fact of nature," so Kegan claims that

> even though our meaning-making activities are richly idiosyncratic, there seem to be things about them that are remarkably regular, and it may be that some kind of acquaintanceship with this life force helps us to be better phenomenologists, helps us better to stand in the shoes of the people that we work with.

In addressing the meaning-making activities of adolescents forming values, he urged us to develop some sense of what a student's "growing edge" is and to think about "ways to accompany that journey." Teachers must recognize "the powerful integrity of these meaning-making systems and see this process of developing and changing as a source of adolescents' behavior."

He illustrated his own vivid observation of this process by telling us of his teaching seventh graders a short story, "The New Kid," by Murray Heyert. (The story is included in the 1945 O. Henry Memorial Award Prize Stories, Doubleday, 1946.) Marty subjects "the new kid" to the same kind of abuse he underwent when he was "new." Kegan's seventh graders approved of Marty's behavior and saw it as fulfilling a primitive justice: if you've been picked on, you'll eventually get your chance to pick on someone else. Marty, they thought, behaved in the only "right" way to behave.

Kegan, stunned with disbelief on encountering this response, gradually came to realize that "they were making sense of their experience and that there was a power, an integrity to their sense." And although they could not generate another interpretation of the story, their discussion of it was not an amoral discussion for they appealed to a strong sense of fairness, they were able to take Marty's point of view.

These seventh graders were able to get outside themselves imaginatively and take another person's point of view. The problem was that they were not able to coordinate Marty's point of view with the "new kid's" — they couldn't take both points of view at the same time.

The ability to coordinate points of view signals "the dawn of adolescence from a developmental perspective." In this transformation one first begins to take one's own needs not as "subject" but as "object"; instead of being one's needs, one "has needs and is able to coordinate one's own needs with another's. . . . Every development involves a new kind of overcoming of egocentricity" in the progress toward realizing "interpersonal relationships."

"The question is are we going to join and aid this natural curriculum or impede it." The "heart of teaching" is learning ways to be useful to students in this meaning-making activity. The perceptive teacher sees that this process is "not just an accretion or a new thought or something which is added to what students thought before, but actually involves a kind of evolution or transformation of who it is they themselves are."

There was one student in that class of seventh graders who began to question the class's categorical support of Marty; and this student, Kegan discovered, was probably "going to be the moral educator in the classroom. My role, I saw, was to keep channels open so that this student could be heard." This student was in his meaning-making changing the construction of subject and object:

what before was "subject" was becoming "object." He was beginning to take a perspective "not just of a relationship, but of a group as a whole, of a society": "where subject was, there shall object be." And the teacher's role is to recognize such potential "moral educators" among the students, to signal to them that they are being heard, being understood.

So, in addition to trying to point out to you some of the consistency or wholeness of these regular world views of one's values, I've also been trying to suggest to you something of the process that I observe in making transitions from one world to the next because they don't just happen between Friday and Monday.

VII

PROMOTING MORAL ACTION THROUGH MORAL EDUCATION

Joseph Reimer

If a school mathematics teacher were asked why he teaches algebra or geometry, he might respond that although many of his students may only have rare opportunities to use that knowledge later in life, learning the skills involved may help them to think more adequately. If a developmental psychologist were able to show that this teacher's math classes promoted students' ability to think in terms of formal operations, we would probably agree that the teacher had achieved his stated goals.

When students of Piaget's and Kohlberg's theories of moral development began thinking about how they could apply the theories to classroom instruction, they intuitively adopted the same rationale as the math teacher. They hypothesized that if they engaged students in the discussion of hypothetical moral dilemmas, the students may never face those dilemmas in real life, but they might develop skills that would help them to think more adequately about whatever moral dilemmas they will face in real life. As developmental psychologists, they tested their hypothesis by giving students pre and post "Moral Judgment Interviews" to see if the discussion of hypothetical dilemmas would result in students' reasoning at higher stages of moral judgment. In most cases, their hypotheses were confirmed (Rest, 1976).

Moral education, however, is not completely analogous to math education. If a math teacher not only teaches the content of his course well, but also helps to stimulate students' general capacity for formal operational thinking, people do not then hold him responsible for the students' acting illogically in other contexts. Yet people do expect that moral education will affect not only how well students reason, but also how likely they are to exercise their moral judgment in terms of moral action.

Blatt, who was the first of Kohlberg's students to apply moral development theory to classroom instruction, tested for the effects of his classroom program on both the students' moral judgment and moral action. He found that while a semester of discussion of hypothetical moral dilemmas resulted in students' advancing an average of one-third of a stage in moral reasoning, there was no corresponding change in the students' behavior on experimental cheating tests. Even the students who through the program had advanced in moral reasoning were not any more likely to resist the temptation to cheat than they had been before the program began.

Blatt's findings may be disappointing, but, we argue, they are not surprising. His curriculum encouraged students to reflect on hypothetical situations. That should not have had a positive effect on their moral action. Students were being taught to reason; they were not being taught to act on their reasoning.

To achieve the latter goal, a moral education program would have to approximate natural contexts in which people learn to act on their moral judgment. I will describe one such context and try to derive from it principles of operation which could be applied to the design of moral education programs.

A well-known study of the relation of moral judgment to action (in a natural setting) was done by Haan, Smith and Block (1968) at the University of California at Berkeley in the aftermath to the 1964 Free Speech Movement. One of the objects of the study was to test the relation between the students' stage of moral reasoning and their decision either to join or not join the protest movement. The hypothesis was that since the primary issue involved was whether it was right to take an illegal action to uphold the principle of the freedom of speech, students who reasoned at the principled stages of moral judgment should have been more likely to have joined the protest than students who reasoned at lower stages.

The hypothesis was confirmed by the data. The students who reasoned at a principled level on Kohlberg's hypothetical dilemmas were far more likely to have joined the protest than were lower stage students. The students least likely to have joined were those who tested at the conventional stages of moral reasoning, with the transitional students occupying a middle range. The students at each level seemed to have acted in accordance with the logic of their stage of moral reasoning.

In reviewing this study at Berkeley, Roger Brown (Brown and Hernstein, 1975) raises a question which is central for our concerns. What was it about the Berkeley situation that promoted a general consistency between students' hypothetical moral judgment and moral action?

Brown's question reminds us of the hazards we would encounter if we were to broadly generalize from the Berkeley context and conclude that this study proves that people generally tend to act on their highest stage of moral judgment. For while the Berkeley situation may not have been unique, it had specific characteristics which other contexts do not share. To enumerate a few of these characteristics: (1) The Free Speech Movement's sit-in was preceded by months of public and private discussions among people of different moral stages. The discussions allowed for a thorough exploration of the facts, principles and consequences involved in the situation. Students had ample opportunity to arrive at their positions. (2) The administration acted in a fairly arbitrary way by banning all political activities on campus. That set up a situation in which the issues involved were perceived as fairly straightforward. (3) Because the controversy engulfed the campus, it was hard for students not to feel involved in the situation. The levels of moral concern and involvement were high. (4) Those who chose to protest were not acting as isolated individuals, but as part of the movement which evolved ideological norms for action. The norms of sitting in to protest an infringement of individual rights were, I assume, structured by principles of moral judgment. The group's norms, then, reinforced the individuals' tendency to act on their highest stages of moral reasoning.

To list these characteristics is not to belittle the significance of the choices made by the students. Only a minority of the students on campus chose to protest, and those who sat in did so at the cost of getting arrested by the police. I believe, as do Hann, Smith and Block, that the students' levels of moral judgment played a major role in the decision process. But I agree with Brown that the specific characteristics of the situation made it more likely that students would act on their highest stages of moral judgment. Had there been less time to discuss the issues, less pull to get involved, less clarity about the choices involved and less opportunity to act in concert, I believe there would have been a weaker relationship between moral judgment and action.

While we cannot and would not want to recreate in moral education programs the exact characteristics of the Berkeley situation, we learn the following from its example: (1) when a controversial issue of moral significance arises on a school campus, its public discussion

— if handled wisely — can be of educational significance; (2) students should be given opportunities to form and express opinions on issues of school-wide concern and even to form groups that advocate certain positions; and (3) whenever possible, students should be encouraged to act on their judgment, to make sacrifices for their beliefs and to take the consequences of their action.

In regard to the third point, the Berkeley example is probably the least informative for the future. We hope protests against school administrations will not be the main vehicle in the future for expression of moral judgment and passion, but that most school administrations will help make available avenues of action for the achievement of positive social ends. Whatever the specific end may be, the main point is that a proper balance between moral judgment and action will best be attained when we provide our students with opportunities to learn how complex is the process of realizing in action the values and ideals we envision through the facilities of our moral judgment.

References

Blatt, M. and Kohlberg, L. "The Effects of Classroom Moral Discussion upon Children's Level of Moral Judgment." *Journal of Moral Education*, 1975, 4, 129-161.

Brown, R. and Hernstein, R. *Psychology*. Boston: Little, Brown, 1975.

Haan, N. Smith, M.B. Block, J. "Moral Reasoning of Young Adults: Political-social Behavior, Family Background and Personality Correlates." *Journal of Personality and Social Psychology*, 1968, 8, 239-253.

Rest, J. "The Research Base of the Cognitive Developmental Approach to Moral Education." In T.C. Hennessy (ed.), *Values and Moral Development*. New York: Paulist Press, 1976.

June 24

We met as schools this morning for further discussion of specific programs to suggest to Olsen [Headmaster of Hotchkiss]. We agree on getting an outside person in to get things started. We haven't worked out much of a format for that yet. Also later faculty meetings to evaluate progress. Some kinds of meeting with students (advisees?). Suggestions on new faculty orientation and on hiring policies and practices. Would the latter tend toward more uniformity in faculty?

Also talked about agenda for days with Kohlberg, both as schools and together. Settled on combination of plenary meetings to hear and respond to him, possibly group meetings, and certainly meetings with schools, probably open to observers. Sounds OK.

First week has gone well. We have gotten acquainted, which was the big task of the first two days, regardless of agendas. We have thought and talked about moral education in very abstract and general terms, but at the end of the week thinking was beginning to crystallize into specifics. This may be due to the outside guests, more likely to the passage of time.

I hope next week we (I) will feel more free to criticize the others, whom I now regard as my friends. This week we have let each other get away with too many fuzzy ideas and jargon and poorly defined terms.

The writing day was a brilliant idea. That was probably the most productive single thing we did.

June 26

Kohlberg's interest seemed basically in direction of use of cases in classroom. Showed tape of teacher using A Separate Peace to initiate moral discussion. Goal is to get some kids to move up a level, which is fine. Question of democracy came up again and he didn't back off from the position that this is the only basis upon which a just and fair community can be built. We certainly aren't there.

Good things — I suppose I did pick up a couple of new ideas today; about smaller democratic groups in an overall nondemocratic institution; ideas on using dilemmas in my ethics course.

Best thing was actually throwing the Heinz case at us for a discussion.* This is the first time we have really had to take a stand in front of our friends on a real (if hypothetical) moral issue. And we could argue about it. I think if something like that had been programmed into the Institute at an early point we all would have been much clearer about our tasks. It's been easy to say, "Well, we all have different standards, but we can agree on thus and such." It really breaks down fast under the weight of a specific case. We each want to take a stand we can defend and then convince others of the correctness of our stand. I don't think any of us is as tolerant as we let on.

*A hypothetical moral dilemma formulated by Kohlberg for classroom discussion.

VIII

SUMMARY OF LAWRENCE KOHLBERG'S OPENING REMARKS

Lawrence Kohlberg had, of course, been informed by his colleague Joseph Reimer of the focal points of our deliberations in the Institute. When he first spoke to us, he observed that he was confident in dealing with the didactic side of moral education, specifically "the ways in which moral issues can be discussed in the classroom"; he was, he said, "more cautious about giving advice" about the moral atmosphere of a school and matters of governance although he recognized, as in his own Cluster School in Cambridge, such concerns make for a powerful force in moral education.

He spoke about his theory of stages in moral development, and he noted that despite what his detractors assert, he feels "the stages are a fact of nature." An awareness of the stages "allows a better understanding of the individual student and it will very often allow people to understand why communication is not taking place. That's probably the greatest and most obvious advantage of knowing about the stages." Often the student "processes what you're saying through his own lenses." He noted parenthetically that "not only individuals but communities can be described in terms of stages," that in the Cluster School they had noted some progress in the community.

He spoke of his overriding conviction that "the very nature of morality is such that it leads us to seek universals"; in asking us to discuss his familiar Heinz moral dilemma he wanted us to see that "everybody involved in moral education has to cope with the issue of the relativity of values." And this is a critical point for secondary school teachers because our students are so often moving out of conventional stages into a way station of relativity, a temporary period of amorality: they detect the arbitrariness of conventional morality, but they do not yet discern the principles beyond conventional morality.

The following three excerpts indicate the line of argument in his concluding remarks:

> If there's a direction in which human beings are going, then one's job as an educator is to provide the conditions that help students to move in that direction rather than to let them stay where they are. If you're going to have any effect on students at all, it will always be in the developmental direction.

> Moral development seems to me the basic aim of moral education; not the only one, but by moral development I mean helping students to move to the next stage in their judgment and reasoning and also translating that stage of reasoning into action, which is a more complicated question.

> If development is the aim of education, then to some extent democracy must be the means of education, or what I call the articulation of a just community.

IX

SUMMARY OF SCHOOLS PRESENTING "WHAT DO WE DO RIGHT?"

At our second plenary session Thomas Quirk, Vice Rector of St. Paul's School, suggested that we have a presentation from each of our schools identifying those programs that have been successful at our schools. Those presentations, a summary of which follows, offered a tonic for the slight malaise we acquired in reflecting on how far we fall short in creating a sound moral atmosphere at our schools. When we offered these observations on "What Do We Do Right," Professor Kohlberg was present and his observations on what he heard follow this summary. Karl Roehrig of Andover spoke rather movingly about his response to the presentations from each school:

> The only false perspective is the one that comes to believe it's the only one there is. So I think that a conference like this in sharing as we have been today helps all of us to get a larger grasp on the reality and the truth of all our schools.

Mr. Roehrig considered that many of the programs going on in our schools can be extrapolated as moral education and therefore as "forces for humanizing our schools."

It was of course natural that the presentation focused some attention on those aspects of school life that obviously make for a cohesive sense of community and a discernible moral atmosphere. Assemblies of the entire school, in some schools once a week, in others as frequent as three times a week, were thought to be most effective: in the words of one participant — "We do get together." Occasional schoolwide symposia and conferences on topics such as leadership and moral education also generate a strong sense of community. Some schools consider chapel services — both required and optional — distinctly worthwhile and argue the value of trying to achieve a subtle unity in formally recognizing the religious pluralism of the student body by appointing school ministers of different faiths — as, for example, at Andover where there is a Catholic, a Jewish and a Protestant chaplain. Some schools referred to the deliberate attempt to involve faculty spouses in such activities as sitting on community councils in the school and attending faculty meetings. And in our cafeteria age some schools pointed proudly to "sit-down meals" — occasionally in some schools, frequently in some others. All of these programs augment, in varying degrees, a sense of community in our schools.

Pre-school conferences for the faculty, regular faculty meetings, and extensive faculty meetings at which each student's career in the school is reviewed as at Hotchkiss were identified as useful gauges of the moral climate. Informal faculty discussion groups and an "open door" administration can build a sense of colleagueship, of professional stature and of effectiveness in individual faculty members. Most participants agreed that these modes of communication within a faculty create opportunities for seeing the totality of teachers' and students' experience in the school.

Student involvement in decision-making and in serious reflection on the values of the community can be a most effective way of developing responsibility and leadership. In some schools students are voting participants in disciplinary cases, in some they can send representatives to faculty meeting, in some students actually have a role in determining the agenda of faculty meetings, in some they have a role in determining financial decisions and even hiring decisions, in some they have a role in admissions policies and decisions. Students do have some part in the governance of the institution.

Four areas — counseling, special courses (both required and optional), alternative study programs and community services — appear to be especially significant for helping the student integrate his or her emotional, social and moral life with an academic skills-oriented routine.

Whether a school has full-time counselors, part-time counselors, or consultants in clinical psychology or psychiatry, there appears to be a universal effort in the seven schools to demystify the counseling process and to provide support systems which students can trust. In general our schools want counselors to have a different status from teachers and administrators so that they are not perceived by the students as any kind of adjunct to the "official" system. They take active part in the life of the school — in coaching, for example — but beyond individual counseling they consider themselves most effective when they help organize and lead strictly optional programs such as those on peer counseling and proctor workshops. They can, and do, help enormously in meetings with teachers and advisers on students who are in stress. Counselors, a school physician and various medical consultants meet regularly with deans in some of the schools.

Several of the schools have special courses of varying rigor, most of them optional, studying human development, human sexuality, physiology, ethics and traditional courses in religion. There was an interesting debate in the Institute on the viability of a special course in human sexuality at an all-male school: some participants assumed that there would be unusual resistance to such a course in a monosexual setting; others, especially those participants from Deerfield, pointed out that the reverse was in fact true, that there is an explicit student interest in such a course. There appears to be a paucity of the Kohlbergian kind of course focusing specifically on moral dilemmas. The Lawrenceville team spoke of the efficacy of an Outward Bound program within the school, a program which not only tests the courageous but affirms the considerable strengths of the less athletic students. This program also builds a fine bond between faculty and students as does a work program where the clichéd polarized relationships between teacher and student get "nicely blurred."

Alternative study programs can emancipate a student from the rather myopic elitist context of our schools as can some of the well-established programs which involve students in services to the larger community. Such programs, in the words of a participant, produce "some very touching human relationships."

It might be useful as a kind of summary to refer again to one of Karl Roehrig's remarks: "Sharing our power with students has been the toughest thing we've had to come to deal with." That observation probably holds true for all our schools; and it is, to a large extent, the dilemma that Lawrence Kohlberg addressed in responding to our presentations.

June 27

Afternoon there was time to write, and I did a scissors-and-tape job on Steve's and my letters to put them together. I hope the three of us will be able to get together and put it into a form we can all buy.

Kohlberg responded to what he has learned for 45 minutes this afternoon. Talked about three levels (ideal, practical, personal) and still maintains that democratically-run school is best for teaching democratic virtues of justice and responsibility. Also talked about our schools in four areas — classroom moral ed, counseling, administration and dorms — which he feels could be a context for practicing democracy.

Best time for me was conversation with Kohlberg over breakfast. Talked about teaching ethics, combining ethical theory and cases or dilemmas. He suggested I get his dilemmas and test class at beginning and end to see if anyone moves up. I will write for the materials when I get home (Cambridge 02138). He is really good in conversation. I am really taken by his schema (stages). Even if it isn't as cut-and-dried as his articles let on, it is a very useful analytical schema. I wonder if anyone has tried to use it as an analytical schema for historical development. Kohlberg also mentioned a divinity school researcher who is finding analogous stages of religious development. K.'s research is now turning to the moral atmosphere of schools and impact on moral development (Cambridge Cluster School) and on the family impact in moral development.

Kohlberg's presence was a huge plus for me.

X

RESPONSE
Lawrence Kohlberg

Let me at least start out at the blue sky level, the level on which the basic kind of commitment to doing something further in moral education exists — that is, democratizing the schools. Let me explain why I think that is basic now, even if it wasn't basic a generation ago. I'm not saying it's urgent, necessarily, but I think it's inevitable in the long run. Traditionally, preparatory schools have had as a purpose the preparation of some kind of moral and civic leadership, and, in fact, they've been reasonably successful for long periods in the past in making good that claim. When I went to Andover, that rationale was still preached and preached in some notion of *noblesse oblige*, of exercising some role of service in the society when we got out. I myself feel that my generation getting out of Andover didn't really fulfill that, and I would include myself as much as others, and we had a pretty high level of talent and intellectual ability and interpersonal skills. But when I go to my class reunions, I don't get a great sense that we've contributed much in the way of moral or civic leadership at any level in the generation that we've been adults. I think that there was a tradition of moral leadership and service which, as I say, independent schools to some extent served within a more traditional autocratic conception, because benevolent autocracy is certainly compatible with high moral character and with integrity and caring. But I think of the tradition of Boyden at Deerfield and that era is dead, and today if we want to think about any of our students exercising moral leadership as adults, we really have to think of them as being democratic leaders or leaders in a democracy rather than in an autocracy. I don't think we can say that leadership will continue to be a Boyden, a benevolent and moral autocrat breeding more

Boydens, who will then breed more schools of benevolent and moral autocrats and so on. I don't think there's going to be much of a place for that kind of leadership in our society. Moral leadership has to be leadership that generally operates in a much more broadly democratic framework, one that can cope with change. And I don't see how schools can at all help to educate for leadership in a democracy unless they're democratic themselves. I know it's very difficult to do that; but I don't really think it's the task of the family to do that; I don't see how the family can do that. I think in the ideal sense the residential school is the place for students to experiment with making and remaking a community, a society, that is beginning to exercise some moral responsibility and leadership. Yet it's difficult.

We say the kids are too young for democracy, and yet we send them out into the world at 18 when they're supposed to be adult citizens living in a democracy. Doesn't that process have to start earlier than 18? I'm not trying to say that an autocratic system is unfair or immoral or inhumane; in fact, the best reason for autocracy is a well-justified belief that adults are able to be fairer or to have a higher level of fairness than kids are. It's really that problem that has preoccupied me in my own work; that is, how do you make a democratic school of kids who are only at the second or third stage of moral development and really don't understand stage five principles? But I would hate to see this Institute not face that issue of democracy, not in terms of practical next steps, but at least to worry through what the ultimate long-range ideals and hopes might be—and whether there is any way to implement them.

One thing that I stressed yesterday was democracy, the Dewey approach, and I think that the second thing that I tried to stress, and I would hate to see it totally dropped, is the importance of getting students, and faculty members for that matter, to think very hard about what's right. That's what Socrates did, after all — to keep pushing people to think hard about what's right. It's as difficult as democracy; we even saw that when we began discussing philosophical issues of absolutes, relatives, and so on. But we do want to face the challenge.

My model of the intellectual side of moral education is Socrates and Socrates did nothing but ask questions. One of the things that's sometimes lost sight of about the Socratic approach, particularly in values, is that the reason people took Socrates' questions so seriously was that they knew that up his sleeve he always had that faith in the absolute. It was that sense that there *was* something beyond relativity which I think made people take his questions so seriously. We have to keep thinking with some seriousness about the absolutes that inform the questioning process — otherwise Socratic questioning becomes some sort of easy game like the psychologist or psychiatrist always asking another question.

I did want to disagree with Ted Sizer, then, in his saying that in moral education we can only think about the contextual, or the moral atmosphere of the school. That's terribly important, but I think the academic approach is important because if we let ethics be considered to fit into the clichés people have about sensitivity and human-relations training, touching-feeling stuff, and don't really stress that it's a first-class intellectual subject in an intellectual curriculum and not compensatory counseling only, we are in trouble. I think that one has difficulty in getting an intellectually and academically biased faculty to consider it seriously. The kind of courses some of you are teaching in ethics serve some symbolic purpose beyond whatever they may achieve in terms of stimulating individual kids. At least they make clear that they have a place in an intellectually-focused school, that moral and ethical matters are not soft subjects. From my point of view the idea of hard thinking about values and the existence of a democracy go together because there's a certain sense in which you can't ask kids, or even a faculty, to think about what's right if they're thinking part of what's right doesn't go with some power to decide, to make decisions themselves in terms of what's right.

When we start to talk about next steps, I'd like to pick up some things that Karl Roehrig was saying, as well as other people, in which, I think quite appropriately, the name of moral education is really being used as a way of talking about the need for a better balance or an integration among a number of things that go on in independent schools. After all, Plato called a balance of the intellectual, the emotional and the appetitive, justice. So we can call that kind of integration of the personality moral justice, if you like. But it certainly involves a balance, an integration, and I think what in various discussions of the last two days we were saying is that there is a division: there is a counselor with a focus on the emotional, an academic with a focus on the intellectual and an administrator with a focus on behavior. Obviously we are dealing with a whole person but the way we approach him from behavior can be in one set of terms, the way we approach him intellectually in another set of terms, and emotionally in a third set of terms. So that there's really an obvious need not only for the kid to be integrated, but for the counselor, the administrator, the teacher, to be integrated. Maybe before we talk about integration for the students, we have to talk about whether an ideal faculty member should have some ability to be a counselor, an intellectual, and a democratic and fair administrator. I think that's a ridiculous ideal, that is, that teachers have to be moral heroes — I don't say that every faculty member in an independent school is going to be a mixture of Socrates, Carl Rogers and Abraham Lincoln. But at least we have to think about those things.

I was struck today by the fact that there are a lot of convergences in your practices, and it seemed to me that if there were enough convergences that maybe you might want to consider little committees or task forces that would deal with these areas of convergence. Let's take first, perhaps, something that emerges out of the counselor role, a focus of interest in a number of schools. There seemed to be a trend to getting a counselor to deal with some issues of curriculum — certainly the development of courses in human sexuality with some ethical concern in terms of interpersonal relationships.

A second convergence seemed to be an interest in counselors becoming involved in doing some teaching or exploring of peer counseling, which certainly seems to me a very good way not only of providing kids with some more help than they can get in individual counseling but really in terms of the cultivation of what Ted Sizer refers to as compassion. I think that there's no better way of cultivating that virtue than getting kids to stop and really try to listen and to see things from the point of view of another person. There are studies showing that peer counseling stimulates kids' levels of thinking on moral issues more than a didactic model of discussion would.

Then a third convergence seemed to be the involvement in school governance and the moral atmosphere — things like groups for training proctors, which, of course relate to interest in peer counseling, but which seem also to move into moral issues about the connection between peer relations and confidentiality and obligations to the school community, which are matters for moral discussion. So these kinds of moving of the counselor role from a firefighting approach to something more like positive educational functions blur the distinction between counseling and education, and seem to me a very good thing to do from the point of view of integrating the elements of moral education.

Another trend that bore more discussion and mutual thought was that of the programs and plans for community service — both a kind of work service within the school as at Choate-Rosemary Hall and community service at Deerfield in terms of Alternative Study Programs. Again, I think those things would bear directly on some virtue of service such as Ted Sizer was talking about. I think that it's important to make those forms of alternative work and study be morally educative. I do think it's helpful, of course, if there's a context of deliberate discussion of moral dilemmas arising from such programs.

The entire school level is obviously very difficult. I think we've heard of a number of situations of experimenting with participation without much power — that is, when students can come to speak in faculty meetings or disciplinary committee meetings where they are not necessarily empowered. I do think that that does serve a number of useful functions, or at least can, and it's better than not having that kind of participation. It does build awareness and communication, and it does breed a better understanding by the students of the faculty's point of view and their reasoning, and vice versa, and I think it does contribute to an atmosphere of more trust between students and faculty.

I've heard about different experiments — this new one at Choate-Rosemary Hall of a "limited override" and so on — that are interesting. But it's clear that whole-school democracy is not around the corner and this gets us back to what is really the unit at which maybe this integration should occur. That is, the integration of counseling concern for student feelings and problems, administrative concern for fair rules and discipline, intellectual concern for thinking about questions of rightness and justice. And it strikes me from talking to different school groups that the most valid unit is the dormitory or house, — that's maybe the only feasible unit of integration. If only dormitory heads or housemasters really had the resources and energy, they could see that all these things went on at the house level. There could be auxiliary courses with ethical implications like sexuality and human development courses or regular ethics courses as house courses. Or there could be the kind of peer counseling discussion of personal issues. There could be the discussion of rules and discipline at the level of a democratic community. In most cases there is at least some autonomy at the dormitory or house level where some scope exists for making a few rules within a context of institution-wide rules and in terms of interpretation of rules and discipline.

That seemed to me the most feasible unit and perhaps the unit where some movement toward decentralization of things now centralized can occur.

I think that leaves us with the question that may be the major practical problem with moral education: the lack of an institutionalized definition and recognition of a role for people involved with social, emotional and moral development.

In Israel, for instance, in the kibbutz boys' schools, adults have two functions: one function is called teacher, another function is called *madrich*, which translates into group leader, counselor, dormitory resident. And the *madrich* usually does some teaching — doesn't always, sometimes his is a full-time job — but generally he is the person of the highest prestige in the educational setup in a kibbutz because it's felt that he has the real responsibility, the ultimate responsibility for the students.

I'm just suggesting the situation in which a dormitory head may get, if he's lucky, one less course to teach, or a lighter coaching load and some financial benefit—an institutional commitment to that kind of role. And it seems to me that there should be a serious commitment to experimenting with taking that role seriously and giving housemasters the energy and freedom to work with one another in building a philosophy of this kind of work. That would appear to me a basic need if some of the trends that people seem to be interested in here are to be feasible.

June 28

Douglas Heath here today. There couldn't be a stronger contrast with Kohlberg. Talked for three hours this morning about his current research and interests, which are very diverse, but always got back to his model of maturing. Captivating speaker/teacher.

During the afternoon he met with individual school groups. He was very helpful with us, mostly confirming what we have already decided plus giving us some ideas for ways to convince faculty of need for the discussions we propose.

Evening sessions on teaching principles (again based on his model of maturing process) — very helpful in making me conscious of things I don't think about, but should. Even a few things I already do. Second session was description of his evaluation of a prep school of about the size of Hotchkiss. Detailed but very suggestive of things we could think about when evaluating our own goals.

I feel that there is much more to say about Heath, but I haven't digested very much yet. He strikes me as a diagnostician of sick schools. Kohlberg is more like the medical researcher.

Heath is very exciting to listen to and everyone is pretty enthusiastic. I feel myself wanting to look to him as the dispenser of magic formulas, however.

XI

SUMMARY OF DOUGLAS HEATH'S PRESENTATIONS

"*And* if there's one message that I think you can take back to your colleagues, it is to help them not to think dichotomously." That statement and his emphasis on doing much more in the classroom than our contextually-oriented Institute had so far encouraged us to do constituted Douglas Heath's major points. "We polarize": "The counselors are over there and the academic faculty are over here as if they have no relationship, as if they're not helping each other." We tell our students not to think dichotomously, not to separate values from intellectual pursuits, and yet we do that very thing ourselves. We put the academic in opposition to everything else: "values, affective education, interpersonal skills." "We must empower a teacher to create a more effective classroom atmosphere in ways which will help further not just academic but also character development."

And it is of "character development" rather than of "moral education" that Heath chooses to speak because he wants to emphasize much more than simply "a specific value position or a specific way of approaching a value question"; these kinds of issues are intimately related to something that subsumes them, namely maturity.

Heath wanted to give us a background on what he sees happening to students — students, he reminds us, we are likely to get in our schools — in order to help us anticipate some of the changes we might well have to make. He pointed out the constant observable passivity, boredom and apathy in students — particularly way down in kindergarten and elementary schools. Saturated with the experience of television, those students "expect to be entertained." It is so much harder, teachers say, to get students to participate in class now. A-five-year-old says to his teacher: "I'm bored. What should I do now?"

Even experiential programs such as "Outward Bound" are finding a "regression in adventuring." In the face of this deepening kind of passivity we must begin to anticipate the educational consequences if these trends continue. "You are going to find that some of your traditional teaching techniques become increasingly less effective."

Even more alarming than boredom, however, is the growing trend toward violent, aggressive behavior among students. The cruel "put downs" have worked their way into elementary school: calling a classmate a "faggot" becomes a principal means of communication. "What does that do to kids? What does that do to their educability?"

With this grim background in mind, we must be sensitive to where change in our institutions can occur. Students' pathetic passivity and desperate aggressiveness seem to point to their growing dissatisfaction with the pursuit of autonomy. They are beginning to see something fulfilling in corporate identification; there is a beginning acceptance of this, a growing psychological openness to authority. "Youngsters need adult articulation of students' difficulties in establishing relationships with each other and sanction for doing something different."

Heath presented an example of how this direction might be followed in a classroom. On the opening day the teacher asks if anyone has never been "put down." When their silence enables them to recognize this universal experience, the teacher asks how it feels to be "put down." "Terrible," is the inevitable response. "Then," says the teacher, "can we have a contractual agreement that there will be no 'put downs' in this class? Can we agree that there's no such thing as a stupid question or comment in this class?"

And in a boarding school, of course, this articulation of problems and the sanction for dealing humanely with them can extend to the residential life. "Residential schools have the unique opportunity to provide some deep caring for those students whose parents' permissiveness has created intense needs for some meaningful caring relationship with adults as well as other students."

In presenting his theory of psychological maturity as being totally congruent with the major effects of a liberal education, Heath pointed out time and again that "You can not evaluate the effectiveness of your institution independently of what the long-term effects are. You must determine whether the growth you see in your students is really integrative or whether it is inducing strains and stresses that are going to come out later." "Moral education" is really developing psychological maturity, developing character, developing the right hemisphere of the brain as well as developing the left hemisphere and integrating both. "Excellence," as schools often define that pursuit too narrowly, can lead to a distortion of personality.

Psychological maturing is the effect of the "process of adaptation." And since no meaningful change in values can occur without confrontation with a problem, "What are the kinds of supports you put into your institutions to allow a student to tolerate frustration, anxiety and pain while he's beginning the adaptive process to deal with them? That's where a lot of us fail."

We must teach students that the core of the adaptive process is learning how to assume another's point of view; and this skill is of course a major by-product of a traditional liberal education.

Faculties aggressively devoted to academic excellence overlook the whole person, and they will not discover the narrowness of their attitudes unless they follow up the lives of their students in years beyond formal education.

The critical question is: "How are we teaching in the classroom to maintain our academic integrity, but at the same time to create the conditions which are going to help further the development of those youngsters in other ways as well?" Heath emphasizes the appropriate strategy for realizing this goal: don't go about it by talking about values; don't let your faculty think you are undermining the basic academic commitment. "Go along with the teachers' basic identity as scholars, as people working with the mind, and say we think you can be more effective in achieving that basic goal of yours if you will also take into account these other kinds of qualities and teach for them in the classroom."

Another important reality to remember in trying to effect a change in a faculty's attitude: "Sometimes where there is the greatest resistance there is also the greatest potential for change. Don't fight with them; go in the direction they want to go and then turn them in the direction you want to go. But you first must meet them where their commitment is."

"The nemesis of much of our teaching is that what sticks for a while, that which we assess in the classroom, does not generalize, does not persist, over and beyond the classroom." College students, for example, cannot use the calculus they learned in school in a college physics course: there is little transferability of that skill, no capacity to generalize that skill, and "meaningful growth does not occur unless it becomes autonomous and demonstrable in situations other than that in which it is learned."

The transferability of skills becomes the major instrument in the transformation of character. "We want to transform a student's character, not just turn out the same person with more knowledge." One of the great rewards of a liberal education is not only that it keeps values alive and therefore is "a source of hope," but also that it enables one to learn the adaptive process and the skills of transferability so that the student can adapt to more than one moral situation. And it is the adaptive process that leads one to a core of values common to "the good life," common to the values of the great religions. In fact, it is not revelation but an empirical rationale that leads one to this sense of a core of values and accounts for the present trend in the social sciences away from cultural relativism to the universalist point of view.

Heath was emphatic in pointing out to us that "all your proposals so far in the Institute are ignoring the classroom." He was aware of Sizer's emphasis on the contextual approach and its focus on the twenty-four hour contact with students in boarding schools, and he was aware of Kohlberg's more recent concern for contextual rather than didactic moral education. "Yet," he averred, "the classroom is also a central experience, the place in which value development and character education can go on." A classroom affords the opportunity to take into account other people's points of view, and the more tolerant students become, the more mature they become. The teacher should provoke value-related issues as well as help students articulate them in the classroom. In confronting students with their own values, a teacher can point out those students' difficulty in genuinely listening to the values of each other. He or she must "clarify expectations as to how a person is to grow and be models of the goals that a teacher wishes his or her students to achieve."

And such efforts could conceivably enhance the climate of trust in the classroom, a climate so necessary to create in the opening weeks of a course. The teacher can talk about his own values, too, as a way of creating trust, and students will respect that willingness to be open, even vulnerable. That is one way of encouraging students to feel comfortable talking about their values. (Quaker schools, Heath points out, have institutional sanctions for this openness.)

Students need to learn how to help each other engage in corporate teaching. Such forms of learning may increase their ability to listen to each other. When students can take "alternative roles" in talking to each other, they begin to learn empathy, which, so much a part of the adaptive process, is critical to the development of more mature values.

Heath kept reminding us that we must assess the effectiveness of our schools and judge the worth of our communities by reference to what happens to our students when they leave us for college and eventually for their careers. How well, in other words, have we created the opportunity for our students to attain maturity?

In the face of increasing pressures to demonstrate that we are actually achieving the goals we assert in our catalogues, faculties need to develop on-going methods of self-evaluation, but how sensibly are we preparing our students for college and for the world of the 21st century?

It is, he asserted, difficult to tease out what effects are primarily maturational and what are attributable to the environment of the school as we try to measure how the student is changing. Nevertheless, there are ways to help a school carry out its own evaluation, assuming, of course, that such an evaluation is genuinely motivated to seek guidelines for change if necessary, rather than another routinely going-through-the-motions effort not anticipated to have any effect whatsoever.

In the first place, a school must find different ways to understand its ethos. Multiple points of views are essential in attempting to determine what kind of community the school achieves. And a school cannot proceed with such an evaluation unless it knows what its salient goals are, and knows them in clear language, in operational terms. Finally, it must assess its community comprehensively because the specific findings about its effectiveness in achieving various goals cannot really be accurately determined without an understanding of its overall results.

Different constituencies in the school — from alumni to the newest ninth grader, from the chairman of the trustees to the custodians — can be asked to evaluate the ethos of the community: they can check a list of adjectives — Heath has used a list numbering two hundred — which they believe describes the nature of the community; and they can be asked to check those that they wish they could have checked in order to determine the sense of hope in the school. Constituencies can evaluate each other: it is obvious to have the faculty evaluate the student body and vice versa, but there are other possibilities available as well, such as the staff evaluating the faculty and evaluating the student body. With so many points of vantage explored, an institution can get a good sense of its community, and Heath argues, "a good community will have a high degree of congruence in its perception of itself."

Even though the ethos of a school is an elusive concept, the institution can try to discover important data such as how well people know each other. Faculty members can rate their degree of knowledge of individual students and vice versa. "I want to know," Heath asserts, "if there are students being missed by the faculty. You have to have a school in which it is possible for an adult to know every student; that's my functional rule about the proper size of a school." It is so important to get a picture of the students' sense of how helpful, open and caring the faculty is. Heath argues that a school with an enrollment beyond five hundred risks "anonymization" for many of its students.

It is critical to assess the levels of expectation in the faculty and to learn to what degree the adults of the community share certain goals. The faculty can be asked to rate the degree to which published goals are achieved, and they can be asked to list those qualities they would like to see in an ideal graduating student. Following that, they can be asked to list those qualities they think their students will need in college. Then they can rate how the school appears to be doing in preparing its students for college.

However, Heath points out a much more interesting investigation than observing the discrepancy between what a faculty thinks its ideal graduating student should be like and what they think he or she needs to possess in order to succeed in college: namely, the discrepancy between what they want for their students and what they think the colleges will want. Often, according to Heath, faculties want their students to be compassionate, caring and considerate of others but believe that self-discipline and will are what help students succeed in college. Isn't it true that most of our schools teach students to think, but do not teach them to be compassionate?

We must be aware, Heath asserts, that "the most profound change in our society since the 60's is the emergence of the narcissistic generation." This new hedonism, this sense that everyone has a special right to his self-fulfillment, has meant "the death of communal values." And curiously, this unhappy phenomenon of a new hedonism gets unwitting support from dedicated teachers who too often are so giving to their students that they act as if they are afraid to make demands of them.

We must help our students to carry on their own learning and to be able to transfer what they have learned in the context of a particular course to other intellectual enterprises. We can occasionally publicly ask our classes just how well we are achieving that goal and how well we are helping them develop in the experience of that class into mature people.

And most of all we must cultivate "allocentrism" (always a key term for Heath); we must help our students develop a capacity for warmth in personal relationships and especially for a sense of giving in their lives.

June 29

This was a very full day. Session with Heath this morning on principles and strategies for implementing change. Several good ideas which had come out in earlier contexts but good to see them gathered together.

This was followed by presentations by each school of their plans of action this year. Several schools, including Hotchkiss, plan some sort of workshop to get things going. Some even have very detailed programs thought out. CRH is an example. I hope they don't lose heart when they find some of these will be rejected or blocked. Steve, Blanche and I tried to convey the idea that we couldn't make specific plans without consultation with Olsen. Though that's true, I hope we won't get bogged down in the routine and never really try anything. I appreciated Vince's comment that he wanted to look carefully at his own teaching and the curriculum of his department in light of the school's goals and moral education. We think along the same lines.

Heath responded with a sermonette about the importance of our tasks, of witnessing to our concerns, and also of being very clear about just what our goals are as well as how we plan to get there. This seems to me increasingly the major weakness of the Institute. We have never sat down together and engaged in the kind of moral reflection we expect to teach our faculty and students to engage in. We haven't had a real fight over some ethical issue or dilemma which means something to us. If we had done that early on, I think we would be more clear about what we are doing now.

Heads were here this evening — four of seven, I think. Charlie and Jef summarized the genesis and problems of the conference and Nat gave us all a gentle ribbing — that is the first time I have ever heard anyone pick up the real meaning of Doty. It was a very pleasant evening.

The end of the Institute is dominating us now, I think, even though few mention it. I'm anxious to get home, but there are some people here I will miss seeing every day.

XII

SUMMARY OF SCHOOLS PRESENTING "WHAT WILL WE TAKE BACK IN THE FALL?"

The most passionate assertions in this plenary session were impressive. One participant said that if he'd learned anything from the past two weeks it was that "You can't be afraid of the future." Another participant said that what he had actually confronted in the two weeks of the Institute was himself, or rather his reflection on the kind of model he is for his students and for his colleagues. He went on to say that before he tried to persuade his colleagues back at school of the wisdom of the deliberations at the Institute, he was going to try out many of the ideas in the classroom to see if he could make them work.

His emphasis on the classroom echoed another participant's concern in the final days of the Institute for the specific context of the classroom rather than for the larger contextual scheme we had talked so much about since Mr. Sizer had spoken to us at the opening session. To a certain extent, Douglas Heath's emphasis on the centrality of the classroom brought us to this focus; and to a certain extent, surely, our own awareness of our calling as teachers brought us to it. Whatever the cause, it was clear that many participants were prepared to return to their schools with a new sense of themselves and of their unique roles in their schools.

Various strategies of providing reflection and possible change included a letter from the participants to their faculty and a "Day of Reflection" which would allow the institution to examine its principles. Some participants saw much merit in getting outside speakers as catalysts for symposia on topics like moral education; some saw the need for enhancing moral awareness in the community by having outside speakers address world problems.

It was asserted again and again that headmasters' support is crucial to any design to affect the moral atmosphere of the community. Not only did we look forward to the forthcoming meeting with our headmasters in order to make them aware of our urgent sense of the need for their strong support, we also spoke of the obvious effectiveness of hiring policies on the future moral climate of our schools.

"How receptive are the faculties to this particular issue right now?" The question reminded us of Douglas Heath's caveat to approach faculties on the terms of their values and to affirm boldly those things we now do at our schools that help create a sound moral awareness and that very possibly enhance academic achievement.

But most participants seem to agree that we must redress the balance of studies and character, that we must "redirect time and energy" to character education and reverse a basic assumption of our past: namely, that our students come to us with sufficient moral awareness and our job is to give them skills to become effective citizens. In the words of one participant: "If we can encourage good decision-making and strong personal relations in our students, then academic education will take care of itself."

June 30

Session with Headmasters this morning. Only three were there: Sizer (Andover), Kurtz (Exeter), McClellan (Lawrenceville). Both Charlie and Jef made presentations of our concern about moral education, really summarizing our work and conclusions and asking for support. Response was quite interesting and moving. Lawrenceville head responded with caution that we be careful what we teach as moral principles. After some more remarks, Kurtz made an eloquent plea for the real need in this area — to educate people who will take moral issues seriously and deal with them compassionately. It could well have been the closing statement of the Institute — it really was, in a way.

XIII

FINAL DAY OF THE INSTITUTE
Remarks to Headmasters in Last Plenary Session of Institute

Charles L. Terry

I want first to tell you of the sense of urgency we of this Institute seek to convey to you: our schools must begin without delay to address the issues we have been addressing for the past two weeks. Why do we feel this sense of urgency?

We have asked you to read Thomas Holcombe's Chapel talk in preparation for this session because we suspect that the kinds of observations he makes about Exeter apply to all our schools. We must go back to our schools determined to redress the balance between academic excellence and the development of character; we must boldly oppose the dichotomizing predisposition in some of our colleagues, a predisposition that Holcomb identifies and that Douglas Heath has commented upon in this Institute. The point of education, as of life, is to integrate the intellectual and ethical elements of our personalities, but we are not doing that in our schools, and we consider such a failing demands a sense of urgency in seeking remedies.

Furthermore, we know the issues we've been confronting are urgent issues because so many of our students face enormous decisions in their future — marriage and work, just to cite two — and because so many of our colleagues, particularly those in dormitories, are anxious and confused by the lack of coherence in the total experience of boarding schools.

We all need to make our institutions whole again; if we don't, we are not likely to survive as institutions. We must train boys and girls to have a strong sense of themselves as ethical beings; moreover, we must train them for a kind of leadership that will heighten our national and international experience and will provide hope for our country and for the world. If we don't assume that responsibility, one might ask who will?

We appeal to you to continue to take courageous stands over and over again on the principles you hold dear and that you want to inform your institution. You can be assured that we in this room will stand up and cheer when you lead faculties to an awareness that academic excellence is empty unless the reason for striving for it is rooted in the intention to develop ethical human beings. And we appeal to you to support us so that we can collaborate with you in a daily effort to win over the unreflective and the cynical in our schools. Help us create an institutional identity in this collaborative effort, a spirit of colleagueship that says, in David Weber's words, "What's on your agenda is on my agenda."

I turn now to three areas in which we have considered that change might well be implemented.

We have talked about the tone of faculty meetings in our schools. Too often it is a tone that vitiates the goals we've been discussing; too often it is a judgmental, not a supporting, tone. "The coin of the realm," one participant in the Institute has observed, "is the highly articulate, witty remark."

Each participant in this Institute has done a fair amount of writing about ways to understand and to improve the moral atmosphere of a boarding school community; that writing is powerful and it represents the kind of reflection that should be articulated in some forum of the school. We hope that we can find new forums in our schools for broadening our dialogue as colleagues, and especially for convincing our colleagues that such dialogue enhances academic excellence.

The second area of potentially salutary change comes under the rubric of time. How do teachers perceive their jobs? It cannot come as news that we often lack a sense of professional, let alone personal, fulfillment because we do not have the time in our busy routine to be fully intentional developers of our students' character. We do not actually have the time to do what Douglas Heath urged us to do in putting creative, imaginative energy to work on making our teaching really effective as a means of developing character in our students. We suggest the radical notion of paying teachers more in time than in money, although we are of course aware of the many controversial issues inherent in such a suggestion.

Finally, in the area of hiring, we submit that the triple-threat candidate or the singularly gifted candidate may no longer be the exclusive best credentials. We need to make clear to candidates our commitment to integrating the intellectual and the moral elements of our lives in the community of the school and abroad.

Summary of Participants' Recommendations to Headmasters
Joseph E. Fellows

1/ We encourage the headmasters to give their colleagues time to present and develop the specific ideas and programs written for each school.

2/ We hope that the headmasters will help their faculties realize that teachers educate morally when they educate intellectually (also that they educate intellectually when they educate morally). Very often we teachers do not intend to teach morals; our aim is to teach chemistry or art or.... Each of us, however, *is* a moral educator, whether he or she wants to be or not. It is better to be thoughtful about it.

3/ We need to be challenged and stimulated so that we will be reflective about our own lives and values. We must help accomplish this goal by challenging others to question.

4/ If we teach what we are, then we must define what in fact we are collectively, as well as individually. We hope that you will support, as much as you can, any attempts to arrive at this definition.

5/ After appropriate searching, we must, as individuals and as a group, send out the message loud and clear, through word and deed, that we stand for something, yet we also must be willing to allow young people, whose values are more amorphous, some breathing room.

6/ We must provide both personal and professional support for faculty members so that they know the school cares about them.

7/ We recognize gaps in our professional training and experience. Many of us, for example, do not have the skills to understand student defensiveness. We need programs of professional development to provide knowledge.

8/ We also need programs, especially for younger faculty members, programs to help create a climate which allows them to commit themselves to our rather traditional institutions, but at the same time permits them to preserve a sense of themselves as people with integrity.

9/ We have continued to ask ourselves if we want to promote autonomous student behavior, or if we want students to accept our traditional values. We support, and hope you will support, any efforts to give students the opportunity to struggle with conflicting values and to determine their own rules within the tolerance of our institutions.

10/ Each of us hopes for a continuing dialogue with you, the headmasters, as we try to realize the goals of this Institute in the years ahead.

Remarks on the Last Plenary Session
Stephen G. Kurtz

I am very glad that these two weeks have gone so well, and it's obvious that they have. There's a spirit here that is unmistakable. Something has happened to all of you, and I shall only try to divine what it is from the few remarks I have just heard.

My private quarrel with Exeter ever since I arrived here is centered upon the things you have been worrying about and discussing. We are confused, I think, because the foundations of our spiritual heritage are basically Christian and have been so badly eroded in our time that we don't know where to go for new ones or in what terms even to express the things of the heart. The central dilemma has always seemed to me the one Saint Paul spoke of when he said that that which I would do, I do not, and that which I would not, I do. And there is no way out in the intellect alone. The Christian position insists that the dilemma can only be dissolved through faith and will, in moving from intellectual discernment to conviction and commitment. And I find it difficult to talk about educating in such terms because many do not comprehend the terms, yet impossible not to, because this is the way I want to talk — because of my own upbringing. I confess to you that in many ways this meeting is the fulfillment of my own purpose in life.

I wanted to open our Bicentennial with serious consideration of our central concern or purpose. Ours at Exeter is spelled out in our Deed of Gift or constitution. We share with Andover an almost identical basic statement of purpose, and I am sure that most of the schools represented here can point to similar statements of high purpose that echo our profession of what it is that we are about. That central concern or purpose is the heart or the spirit and not the intellect.

Generosity of the spirit is what we are about, but who wants to hear that? It's hard to convince ourselves that spiritual qualities are really the main concern when what we really seem to value is how many kids we squeeze into the prestigious universities. What will it profit us to gain the whole world and lose the soul? Trite, but we must say it over and over again. The kind of people I want to train at this school will reflect generosity of spirit, and I don't think I know how to inculcate that any better than you do. You say that you must have the support of the heads of your schools, that it is crucial. I say Amen to what you are trying to grasp even though I recognize that it is inchoate or a matter of feeling — something that tries to find its way out of us and seems so difficult to give birth to.

It reminds me of a boy I knew at Kent when I taught there. I had him in my eighth-grade ancient history class and shared him with a colleague who was as non-plussed as I was at the tortuous mental processes of this boy. "He has a mind that is like a pot of oatmeal," my colleague remarked. "As it gets heated up a few bubbles come bloop, bloop, up from the bottom." So, our ideas and conceptions of things come slowly up to the surface sometimes.

I was asked once to give a guest lecture at a small Presbyterian college in Ohio, and I entitled it "History as a Compassionate Science," doubtless a misnomer but accurate in its reflection of my rising disgust with social science and of history viewed seriously as demographical statistics, a drift that explains my departure from professional historical work at the time. I centered my remarks upon a few famous figures who have had to accommodate themselves to the exercise of power. Not a bad subject for us today either, for don't we take great satisfaction in the number of our alumni who have risen to power in the corporate and financial world? Some of those who have been given power have handled it beautifully. One who did not, however, was Napoleon Bonaparte, who twice deserted his armies after leading them into certain destruction, the first in Egypt and the second in Russia. Napoleon found it essential so often to hurry back to Paris on urgent business to put things back in order after creating disorder throughout his world. The famous painting is not of Napoleon saying farewell to his soldiers but later, to his marshals in resplendent uniforms. But there is still another farewell recorded, that of Napoleon going down the line of his advisers, stopping at Talleyrand for one more small humiliation, tweaking his ear, as was his wont. As we all know, Talleyrand later had his revenge, for while Napoleon was elsewhere, Talleyrand was at Vienna protecting the interests of France.

But I think more often of Lincoln and his ability to communicate the things we are talking about by indirection. One of the great moments in the history of our Civil War was made great simply by his spirit. A group of Methodist leaders from Missouri had come to see him to protest the conduct of the war in their violently divided state. They came and their spokesman read a prepared statement that went very much like this: "Mr. President, Missouri is in tatters, our homes are burned to the ground, our fields destroyed, civil war rages, and it is largely your fault. The policies of your government are a disaster and it all rests upon your shoulders." They went on and on, petitioning Lincoln, who had moved to a window, his back to them to turn the situation around. The blood of their families was on his hands, they concluded. Then there was silence, and the President simply turned around, and let the tears run down his face, unable to say anything. Perhaps it was the only answer he could have given them.

And finally, there was the case of that magnificent human being, Pope John XXIII. A few years ago the Moderator of the American Presbyterian Church, Eugene Carson Blake, requested an audience with Pope John. As it was told to me, Blake was full of good will, John full of good will, but how does the spokesman for Calvinism address the Pontiff? Does he shake hands, bow from the waist? To go down on one knee and kiss the Pope's ring is going further in the name of ecumenical hopes than Blake could be expected to go. As Blake entered the room Pope John rose, walked toward him, and embraced him in a great bear hug.

Power and authority can corrode or they can free the spirit. Perhaps what we are searching for is the spirit of grace, and what we long to do is to live it in our own lives so that we teach it by contagion to our students. Probably I simplify the matter, but I can't make a better response to what I feel in this room this morning.

XIV

A PAPER FROM THE INSTITUTE
Harvard V. Knowles

To me, to ask the question, "can we teach morality?" is irrelevant. Ted Sizer has confirmed in me what formerly were simply nudgings around the heart, unarticulated feelings that seemed to have validity even though, unlike his colleagues at Harvard, I had no data to support my feelings. Immediately, I felt the rightness of his observation that in school moral education goes on constantly whether anyone is aware of it or not. And immediately I saw the wisdom in his belief that we should find out precisely what kind of moral education is going on in our schools and in precisely what kind of context, so that we can begin to exploit deliberately the manifold possibilities for moral growth for youngsters and adults that the environment possesses. Perhaps it does not require objective data to bring us to the belief that what we are as people rather than our expertise in a particular discipline is often the difference between being effective teachers and ineffective ones. Nevertheless we do need to be reminded again and again that the kind of people we are, the kinds of decisions we make and how we make them, the language we use in describing each other, the way we react to each other are some of the most important elements in shaping the environment we create for our students. All schools are nurturing environments and therefore it is encumbent on us to know precisely what kind of environment we have produced in order to know what kind of nurturing we are doing. We have to operate on the assumption that what kind of people we are determines what kind of school we are.

We do not live long in a boarding school before we realize that professional responsibilities should not end once we have left the classroom; indeed they only begin there. Because we are in a boarding school we must be willing to be responsive not only to the intellectual needs of our students but to their emotional and moral ones as well. We must take seriously the charge of nurturing implicit in the concept and organization of the residential school. We must be open, generous, responsive and affectionate. We must be patient and long-suffering enough to stay with students through their struggle with themselves, and often even with us, and help them find ways of being comfortable with that emerging self which in the first flush of discovery can be terrifying in its novelty. We must respect our students' wholeness, not fragmenting it to deal solely with their heads. Rather we must discipline ourselves to see them as individuals, to be comfortable with them as growing people that they might learn to be comfortable with themselves. We must be willing to accept that no one is just a student, that reading and writing skills alone are not enough, that learning is not wisdom. Our commitment to our students must be complete, and we must be deliberate in the total environment we create and continue to shape by our presence.

If we can reach across the generational and educational gaps that seem to separate us and concentrate more on sharing the common experiences that bind us together, we will find that our shared laughter, our shared grief will foster a richer environment for moral education. I suppose that the acts of strangers can have a moral impact on us, but I have faith that those we live with, care about, love will affect us more deeply because they affect us in so many different ways.

Our students want us to exert some moral leadership, and they willingly concede that this leadership should have some impact on their lives. Their concession is qualified, however. They do not want our morality imposed on them; rather they want to live in an environment that lets them struggle through to their own moral positions. They want an environment that is flexible enough to allow them to stumble, even to fail, one that stays with them long enough to redeem a wrong decision, an unwise act. In insisting that they want the moral values of their schools to be informed by love, affection, generosity, tolerance, they are reminding us that they are people who need more than academic rigor and football games. They are telling us that they have come to boarding school to live their lives fully, that they are not just students who want exacting academic standards, that they want to be people and not just students. What simple, obvious, and reasonable requests, and yet how easy it is for us as we become encapsulated by our own academic disciplines to forget they are beings whose needs extend beyond the academic and the athletic to encompass as well their passion, anxiety, doubt, confusion.

In school it is easy to become so involved in academic busyness that we forget that academic work is not the full concern of any of us. We sometimes become too self-congratulatory about how many National Merit Finalists we have, how high our SAT scores are, how many students we send to Harvard. Surely, there is nothing wrong with the pursuits of excellence, with instilling in adolescents the desire to stretch themselves as fully as they can to reach goals that at first seemed unattainable to them. We must not, though, become so preoccupied with the end that we fail to see the process which produces it. The moral environment in which achievement takes place is of crucial significance. No school should boast of sending platoons of students to the Ivy League schools if once they get there they are so ruthlessly competitive that they notice their neighbor only to wonder how they can beat him at the academic game. We cannot pursue the winning ethic, which informs so much of education, so single-mindedly that it excludes the realization that one person's victory causes another person's suffering, that achievement is sometimes as much an accident of birth as it is an effort of will or strength of character, but that mercy and pity and justice rarely are. The pursuit of academic excellence is pretty hollow if it is not informed with the awareness that a good mind in and of itself carries no moral value. It is not enough for us to help our students achieve if it does not at the same time help them to see that any of their achievements, and especially those of the highest kind, are measured against the efforts of many others.

Life in school can be so routinized, so structured that it seems to move on its own momentum, sweeping us along in its flow, obscuring at times the complexity of the work we have undertaken in trying to educate other people's children. We must not be so overcome by our concern with our obvious assignment, producing students who are literate, thoughtful, and critical in their thinking, that we ignore the less obvious, the less visible. I submit that our invisible function is often our most important one and yet is the one we are most likely to take for granted. How do we square our wanting them to be honest with their knowledge that we will sometimes fire them when they are? At times this conflict can create an overriding tension in the school. It is how we resolve this conflict, and the many just like it, that will reveal what our true values are, what kind of people we are and consequently what kind of moral environment we are building for education to take place. The students must feel that their efforts, attitudes, desires are a part of the resolution of such tensions. If we ignore them, and construct a legal and disciplinary system that tries to oppose too legalistically and too dispassionately our principles on the one hand and their actions on the other, we may teach and encourage as much dishonesty as we do honesty.

XV

THE RESIDENTIAL SCHOOL AS A MORAL ENVIRONMENT*
Harvard V. Knowles and David R. Weber

Like a good many other faculties ours has a strong sense of its commitments — both to high academic standards and, more broadly, to such humane or moral values as compassion, fairness and courage. At the same time we are aware that many of our students see the school's real commitments in much narrower terms; they would say, if pressed, that the school is chiefly given over to the ruthless, aggressive pursuit of excellence, defined pragmatically as admission to the college of one's choice. These two perceptions, though they are far apart, equally assume that schools teach other things besides their formal subjects, whether they do so deliberately or unwittingly. We share this assumption (as do many other educators) and want to pursue some of its implications. What values does our institution actually reinforce in our students' experience? And how — if we are dissatisfied with the answer to that question — can we alter our school environment so that it will provide a better context for moral or personal as well as intellectual growth?

Students must sense, often unconsciously, that their schools stand for something, that the school's way of life affirms some values and lets others go. Often, however, what is affirmed in practice is not only independent of but actually antagonistic to the faculty's objectives. To attend some independent schools, for instance, is to place oneself within an elitist and monied context when in the country and the world at large scarcity, poverty, and deprivation are widespread. Unless such a school takes pains to complicate its students' social ex-

---
*From *The Phillips Exeter Bulletin*, November 1978.

perience, whether by off-campus programs or by a consistent, dramatic exploitation or other resources, its students may come to accept, or continue to accept, self-centered, complacent premises about their own prospects and role in life. Other schools, in excluding girls, at least risk that their most powerful educational message is that girls, and by extension women, are distracting diversions, destined for separate, presumably subordinate roles. But even co-educational schools whose composition in socio-economic terms is reasonably diverse may say to their students in a variety of subtle ways that personal advancement is the name of their game.

In any case all of us have known students who graduated from our schools with highly distinguished academic records but with minimal interest in other people, with imperceptible commitments to compassion or service. But most or all of us want to work in schools that try to nourish and that *tend* to nourish a less selfish orientation toward life; we want to help create environments which encourage generosity of spirit and principled decision-making, not sophisticated selfishness, in our students and ourselves.

We suspect that one crucial aspect of the moral environment for students at many independent schools is their institution's secularity. (We have no ecclesiastical axe to grind.) A school that identifies itself with a religious tradition of course risks parochialism. But if the religious identification is central and visible and *felt*, not merely formal, it can help the school project more powerfully its deepest value commitments; it can provide a larger moral context for the students' individual strivings. The tradition and its symbols and rites may be experienced as an institutional affirmation of piety, of humility, of commitment to service.

But when the religious underpinning is knocked away, when there is no longer a clear set of religious ideas or values that are centrally and pervasively affirmed by the school, then whatever is left of the ecclesiastical legacy may be perceived by students to be either impotently anachronistic or merely autocratic, constricting, arbitrarily narrow. Exeter's Calvinist legacy is now diluted and secular, if indeed it has survived at all; perhaps it still shapes in some obscure way the school's rather solemn, severe institutional style, the comprehensively judgmental attitude that too many of our students feel weighing on them from the day they arrive. Church services are voluntary, and rather thinly attended; classes are required. The distinction is not lost on the students. (All this is not what we take to be the experience of students at many of the Friends' schools, which seem to communicate a sense of acceptance and respect — and of social mission — along with a high standard of academic expectation.)

Even when the institution's religious identity has been blurred or lost, a forceful institutional personality may still confront the students, only they are apt to hear in its voice the tonalities of the sales-pitch rather than of moral exhortation. A powerful sense of institutional history makes a good many independent schools seem forbiddingly sure of themselves; but the basis of values on which this tremendous confidence once rested is now obscure — except for the history of sustained academic vitality, of achievement, of success in college admissions, of prominent alumni. Sometimes the institution itself seems to be the overriding value; the individual student must prove himself, must conform and succeed, or must conclude that he is worth less than he thought. Institutions like these no longer project to their students a commitment to a set of underlying, truly operative values that could be called religious; instead we project a distinct commitment to another set of values — to excellence, to success, to institutional and personal advancement. The problem is not so much with these values themselves, which can be healthy and productive ones and which may well have as corollaries competence, autonomy, clarity of mind; the problem is that we no longer project any other values — like fairness, or compassion, or a commitment to service, or courage, or honesty or love — with anything like equivalent force.

We would like to turn now to a brief survey of some of the quite specific ways in which schools may unwittingly present themselves to their students as narrowly self-serving. Our focus will continue to be on aspects of school life that tend to be separable from the formal curriculum; but we hope that here as elsewhere it will be clear that we see no necessary conflict between academic seriousness and an effort to be thoughtful and purposive about all aspects of our students' experience. Quite the reverse, for a faculty to concern itself with the affective, moral, or social growth of its students is likely to lead to improved morale, to increased loyalty to the school, and so to a reduction in the motivational failures which limit the intellectual progress no less than the personal development of many students. A good school can be both rigorous and humane.

One of the ways in which a school can misrepresent its own deepest values is through an obsession with its established routine. Life in school can be so thoroughly organized, so structured, that it seems to move on its own momentum, sweeping us along in its flow, obscuring at times the complexity of the work we have undertaken in trying to educate other people's children. We are sometimes so professional, so fiercely committed to the fulfillment of our most obvious assignment — producing students who are literate, thoughtful, and critical — that we ignore the less obvious, the less visible tasks. One of us remembers a day when he was a young teacher and was told on the way to an early morning class of the sudden death of a colleague the night before. The young teacher knew this man well and was shocked, confused, hurt. But being a dutiful teacher he continued to his class, in which he had scheduled an in-class writing, hurrying not to be late. On getting to the class he began distributing the question, passing out bluebooks, trying to settle the class at the same time, readying it for the planned exercise. He knew that the students had heard about the older teacher's death, but he felt that it should be business as usual nevertheless. A couple of students began to murmur that they didn't feel like writing, that this day was different from others and that perhaps the exercise might be postponed until the next morning. After a couple of exchanges the young teacher became frustrated because he didn't want to have to deal with a recalcitrant class when he was still undone by his friend's death. Over the quiet protest of a few he persisted in his plan; the class did go on to complete its task. Their teacher felt uncomfortable in forcing them to proceed as though nothing had happened to them, but he lacked the strength to listen to the class, acknowledge the legitimacy of their reaction to the death of someone close to them, talk it out with them, dismiss the class, do whatever was necessary to help them deal with their pain.

If some of those students recall that class, as their teacher fears they do, their remembrance of it will probably have little to do with its avowed purpose. They are likely to recall that the teacher, by arbitrarily ordering the priorities of the day, denigrated their grief — that the teacher said that writing an essay was more important than the death of a member of the community. Of all the things that this episode might teach us, we want to emphasize one: that how we act toward each other, how we respond to the personal events that impinge upon us as we work, how we live with each other can often be the classroom's most indelible lessons. We must be strong enough at times to deny our academic discipline. Our denial itself, if it stems from an authentically compelling occasion, will not merely affirm our role as adult members of a community; it will paradoxically help our students to see our discipline itself not as an academic chore but as a legitimate human activity that can be integrated into a balanced and responsive life.

Another dimension of school life that can mis-educate students is the faculty's highly visible social style, its manners, its established ways for colleagues to interact with students and with each other. Since adolescents are uncannily skillful at discerning the subtle implications of our example, we must be vigilant that our characteristic actions are consistent with the values we want to inculcate. We all want our students to treat each other with mutual respect, to base their actions on the principle that each individual has inherent worth. We want them to know that manners at some level really do reflect morals. But if we deal with each other with only an overlay of respect and courtly fastidiousness and formality, and then carp and grouse and undercut each other in private conversations with students or in other contexts where students may hear us, aren't we teaching that manners are not morals but rather are superficial ceremonies that we devise to cloak our own unworthy behavior? That may not be what our manners mean to us, but it will be a rare student to whom they will mean anything else.

We should not let some confused idea of respect blind us to our obligations to each other and to the community. To be linked in our daily lives only by a veneer of ceremonial gestures is to say to students that maintenance of the code of behavior matters more than the behavior's inner substance. Should we not seek to be aware of the point at which our professional decorum ceases to be a genuine courtesy, a mark of respect for colleagues and students alike, and becomes instead an unreflective strategy for minimizing anxiety and avoiding important moral questions? What should a teacher do, for instance, when he observes the humiliation of a student by a colleague? Is it truly respectful of anyone simply to look away — or perhaps to commiserate with the student later, in private, or even to intimate to the colleague, disingenuously, that the student was at fault, that the faculty member was only responding to an intolerable provocation? Similarly, should we decline to share our concern with a colleague about his excessive drinking because we "respect" him so much? It is a meretricious respect that disables us as we seek to help each other do better the task we have all set for ourselves. It is true that no one wants to have colleagues who scrutinize and call into question one's every move; and everyone has a capacity for self-righteousness that he must guard against; but we suspect that most of our schools would be better places if faculty members were more direct with each other about their ways of dealing with students, perhaps even about their ways of dealing with each other.

To be constructive, however, directness must be informed by respect, even by charity. Indeed charity, we believe, should be one of a teacher's cherished watchwords. As Hamlet says, we should treat each other better than we deserve: "Use every man after his desert, and who shall 'scape whipping?" We must adopt as our abiding principle a solicitude for the worth of the least attractive, the least popular, the least pleasant among us, for it is only in doing so that we can affirm our belief in the essential humanness of each of us.

This is an injunction more easily stated than followed, we know. But even if we do not always feel charitable towards our students or one another, we can usually push ourselves to *act* charitably. If we want our students to develop the habit of compassion, we must be sure that they are treated compassionately. This is not, we insist, a question of softness versus toughness; it is not a rhetoric devised to disguise an unwillingness to expel students from the school. We happen to think that Exeter has tended to expel too many rather than too few of its students, but we know that there are times when the welfare of the community or even the moral education of the student requires his separation from the school. But that is not the issue here. What we are talking about is professional discipline — a moral discipline the teacher should impose on himself.

One of the ways in which this chosen discipline, this determined charity, is often violated is through our readiness to employ derogatory labels, especially in characterizing students. A student who is respected and cared for will never be labeled a lout, a slut, a loser, a jock — all invidious terms that come too early in too many schools. In creating a negative language we attack adolescents where they are most vulnerable. Not only does labeling deny humanness, it encourages a person to act out the negative behavior that the label seems to demand. It is appropriate that during the civil rights movement of the early sixties, Blacks should have demanded an end to the negative rhetoric that for so long had not only defined the white man's view of them but had also limited their assessment of themselves. Just as negative language had reinforced a sense of Black inferiority, negative language that is used to define students asserts their inferiority.

Such an act has consequences for the user as well as the involuntary recipient of the label. We are too ready to think of each other in terms of one-dimensional roles or other labels, in categories which, like the names of excluded groups, give us a kind of insidious mental shorthand. Just as the racist both demeans the object of his contempt or fear and simultaneously diminishes his own humanity, the same contraction takes place in a teacher given to putting down students. One of the most luminous moments in the Western tradition speaks to this issue categorically. Mary Magdalene was transformed from whore to saint because a great moral leader had the courage to look beyond both label and act, to confirm a person and therefore nourish goodness by embracing what others could only curse.

How, as faculty members at schools that are massively and visibly committed to the inculcation of academic skills, schools that no longer have the living presence of a powerful, shared religious tradition with its symbols and its language and its rituals—how can we convince our students at a gut level that some things matter more to us than the acquisition of skills, than entrance into a prestigious college, than personal achievement, matter more, even, than intellectual autonomy? We do have resources for this task; there may be some value in an inventory.

One level of action is institutional and programmatic. One student attends a school that rarely meets as a school; that has no counselor; that offers or at least requires no course in ethics; whose administration and faculty shy away from anything that resembles preaching. A student at another school attends perhaps three weekly programs that are shared by the whole school community; has the chance to talk with professional counselors or psychologists; spends at least a semester facing in a sustained way (in a course framework, probably) the moral dimensions of personal choices: and can hear the Principal and, say, ten teachers speak publicly from time to time about moral issues of personal concern to them—not in a spirit of handing down the moral law, but in the spirit of bearing witness to what they think and believe. Talks have been given at Exeter—by Richard Sewall, among others—that have changed students' lives for months, perhaps permanently. Most of us will not achieve conversion experiences in our listeners, but we can contribute to their sense that they live with a faculty who think about moral questions, who care about moral issues, and who have positions they aren't afraid to expose. The Principal inevitably bears a special burden. When Stephen Kurtz speaks in an Assembly at Exeter, what happens is not some pointless exercise in adult declamation; what the students hear is both a personal statement and a symbolic institutional commitment. It matters to faculty members, and we believe it matters to the students, what the balance of values is in all these public statements, especially those of the Principal. If the top person were to make a practice of reading letters from alumni who have become successful in law or business and who write to thank the school for teaching them to express themselves clearly, that would say one thing. If instead the top person raises moral issues, issues of value, in a thoughtful way, expressing sometimes his own uncertainties, that says something else. Both students and teachers feel differently about the school and differently about themselves as members of the school community as a result. The students don't want us to be moral autocrats; they do want us to be moral advocates, of a sort. Whether they agree with what we say is less likely to matter than their belief that we speak voluntarily and sincerely. Quaker meeting is not a model that can be exported to non-Quaker schools; but those of us in predominantly secular institutions would do well to find something to take its place.

We should also remember that the moral environment inhabited by any particular student is made up in large measure by the sum of his personal relationships with the people he sees a lot of. In fact two different students at the same school may well have two profoundly different environments. Suppose one has, by chance, the five most respectful, patient, sensitive teachers in the school, and the other the five most "authoritarian" and contemptuous; suppose the one has the wisest and most accessible dorm head in the school and the other has someone who, for whatever reason, resents living in the dorm, minimizes contact between faculty and students, and is consistently unsympathetic to students' problems; suppose the one has a coach who is concerned to foster team solidarity and camaraderie and sportsmanship and the love of the game, as well as the acquisition of its skills, and the other has a coach whose self-image is deeply bound up with the team's won-lost record and who believes in physical contact as an allegory of masculinity, or whose conception of sexual equality is to preach to his female athletes that winning is everything. There is a sense in which these two students do not attend the same school; certainly they are not having the same educational experience. A student perceives his institutional environment one piece—one person—at a time, as well as organically, holistically. Like the school, each of us is a moral educator whether he wants to be or not.

Since the role comes with the territory it needs to be embraced in an intentional way. This conviction need not, however, lead us to stridency, to coercion, to acts of moral aggression. To a considerable degree our charge is simply the avoidance of abuses: we want to recall Hannah Arendt's assertion that "the rules of conscience... [are] entirely negative. They do not say what to do; they say what not to do.... They say: Beware of doing something that you will not be able to live with." Do not let yourself be seduced by the routine, by labels, by a shallow notion of decorum.

What we urge more positively is chiefly a set of perspectives: there is nothing inherently noble in adulthood; there is nothing inherently evil or embarrassing in adolescence. If we see that our students are amorphous, confused, or contradictory, that they sometimes act badly, we should not be deceived into thinking that they are different in kind from ourselves. That they are at a different stage in their development does not make them inferior or less human. Indeed, perhaps we should begin to see that their apparent moral amorphousness is more like our own condition than we are willing to admit. Maybe we are not so much more certain about our moral beliefs as we are more adept at manipulating the rhetoric of morality. If this is indeed the case, perhaps a truly moral educational environment is one that is open to question, that is responsive to the evolving ethical codes of the community, that is secure enough in its sense of its own first principles to entertain questions about values and attitudes. What kind of moral statement does our educational environment make when it implies through the attitude of its teachers that values become fixed with age, that moral behavior, like grey hair and attenuated muscles, comes inevitably with the passage of time? Students should see that a moral position comes from struggle, that it is often expensively wrung from awesomely complex patterns of pain and injustice. To present them a community smug in its assertion of right and wrong, unyielding in its insistence on imposing its values on others, is to present them a model inconsistent with the experience of reflective people. We need to see ourselves not just as teachers but as people; we need to accept our own humanness, our own frailty, our own capacity for growth, as a precondition for accepting our students. We need to help our students see that how we live is our greatest concern.

XVI

NOTES FROM A PANEL DISCUSSION ON DISCIPLINE

DATE: January 31, 1979
TO: The Faculty
FROM: The Principal
SUBJECT: Notes from a Panel Discussion on Discipline, January, 1979

Last Sunday four faculty members and four students joined in a panel discussion of student behavior and the disciplinary system. I had prepared a brief statement that reflected my own conviction that our approach to discipline is largely negative and occupies too much of our corporate attention. Many faculty as well as students attended and participated in the discussion. At the request of a number of the faculty I share my thoughts with all of you. I stress that these are my reactions to and criticisms of our system and not those of the administration. I hope that my ideas will find favor. If they do not, perhaps they will serve to focus our thinking on this vitally important subject as we again take up the report on discipline by the ad hoc committee tabled since last year.

I. PRINCIPLES

In our responses to the misbehavior of our students we create an atmosphere in which all of our relationships are shaped, more so at Exeter perhaps than at any other school because all of the faculty is involved in each serious case. The environment we want is not a matter of concentrated thought, unfortunately, and there is probably no definition of it that would please all.

The system of discipline we support should teach three essential values: honesty, justice and mercy. Even though we may be guided by these values, our students do not perceive it. In this important realm we are poor teachers. They too often see instead harshness, inconsistency, favoritism and greater concern for the system than for the person. One reason for this is that we do not differentiate among the so-called major offenses: drinking, for example, is as harshly dealt with as is deliberate plagiarism.

A. Destructive acts against the community and against other persons should receive stronger punishment than breaches of the rules governing drinking and marijuana. These willful and destructive acts would include wanton destruction of property, physical violence, hazing, lying and stealing (including plagiarism and deliberate misuse of library reserve). To dismiss a boy or girl from the community is a most serious action, and the reasons for doing it ought to be few and far between.
B. Favoritism must be avoided at all costs. Cynicism is bred when one student receives informal warning of what could happen while another, perhaps less personable or less valuable to the community, is charged and dismissed on first offense.
C. Circumstances should be weighed, as is now the case.

II. PROCEDURES
A. Those in authority living in the dormitory with the student under charge should be involved fully with the Executive Committee in assessing the infraction and in voting the recommended penalty, namely, dormitory faculty and proctors. One of the important recommendations of the participants in the Institute on Moral Education was that students be given more responsibility in making moral or ethical decisions as a way of helping them to grow stronger.
B. Penalties should be assigned by this combined Executive Committee-Dormitory Committee rather than by the entire faculty whose role would be confined to supplying new information if there were such.

III. PENALTIES
A. Dismissal — reserved for major offenses as redefined and automatically for drinking and marijuana on second offense.
B. Probation — as applied to drinking and smoking marijuana (as well as other drugs) for first offense but accompanied by a) counseling and b) either a service project and/or suspension to go home. Both Choate-Rosemary Hall and Lawrenceville have lately revived suspension with reportedly good effects. The observation is that parents escape too easily the problem the school is coping with unless the youngster comes home to face them.
C. Restrictions — reserved for lesser rules and regulations, infractions such as lateness, absence, rudeness.

CONCLUSION

We spend an inordinate amount of time on discipline. I repeat that it is in the context of the unhappy business of setting penalties that we most often see one another and act together. We complain that we have too little time for important educational questions as a faculty because of discipline. We refused to hand discipline over to a committee when we reviewed the report of last year's ad hoc committee. I regret that and know that others do. Could we not experiment? Try this system for two years, reverse engines if then dissastified?

Two simple thoughts keep bothering me: what was I like at sixteen or seventeen and how would I treat my own children.

S. G. Kurtz

XVII

SOME REMARKS ON MORAL EDUCATION*
Charles L. Terry

Mr. Callaway and I have a mutual friend at Exeter whom I've persuaded to teach James Gould Cozzens' novel *The Just and The Unjust*. It is a novel about the law; but it is also a novel about how Abner Coates, a decent and intelligent young lawyer, becomes a man of character. He has some help: his friend and boss, Marty Bunting, the District Attorney, says to him in mild exasperation — "Ab, you need to get organized. Why don't you get married?" Abner responds: "I'm sorry, but I don't see the connection." Bunting assures him that there is a connection.

I take this passage in Cozzens' novel for the text of my remarks because I want to argue for a vital connection between two kinds of orientation to our subject that are in appearance dichotomous. And I'll levy on Ted Sizer's language to identify these orientations as, on the one hand, didactic, and on the other, contextual. The didactic orientation includes approaches to moral education as diverse as the school minister's sermon and Lawrence Kohlberg's classroom schema for debating moral dilemmas. The contextual orientation includes approaches to moral education as diverse as a sense of supportive colleagueship among a faculty and positive peer pressure among students.

Why do I want to expose the error of dichotomizing these two approaches?

---

*Delivered at Andover in March of 1979 to the following constituencies of the seven schools represented at the Institute: Presidents of the Trustees, Headmasters and some of the participants.

The trustees of our schools will have to forgive me for making an assumption about how they are approaching our subject this morning. Something within me says that you are thinking about moral education in our schools in terms of powerful didactic reminiscences — not unlike my reminiscenses of the way Mr. Batchelder at Loomis in the late 40's made himself a moral force when he spoke to us in chapel. I don't think Mr. B. often returned to the *Nicomachean Ethics,* but he was surely Aristotelian when he told us boys that goodness was a matter of developing the right habits. I am happy to say this wisdom has stuck with me.

However, Ted, who gave the keynote talk to the Summer Institute on Moral Education, advised us to spend our two weeks examining, not the didactic, but the contextual approach to our subject. We took his advice. We examined the ethos of our institutions. We asked these kinds of questions: The earnest and genuine rhetoric of our catalogue statements aside, what do we really stand for? What values are embedded in the quality of our living? How in our daily routine do we communicate moral principles to each other — faculty to faculty; faculty to students; students to faculty; students to students? We were attempting, you see, not to devise a new curriculum in moral education; we were, following Ted's advice, attempting to learn how we could make effective use of the rich curriculum in moral education that we already have. We have that rich curriculum because the environment of our schools not only enables, but forces, us to live in constant close contact with each other. We have *always* been moral educators: our job at the Institute was to become aware of how we could make ourselves become, and help our colleagues to become, *intentional* moral educators.

Such a contextual orientation to "the goodness curriculum," if you will, focuses on a singularly important moral issue for students nowadays. At least it's important for students at Exeter; I assume it is as important for students at all our schools. The consequences of honesty: that is the issue. Isn't it better, that is more prudent, students are saying, to lie or to refuse to tell the truth because telling the truth only gets one convicted? What is our answer to this question?

I have two answers. My first answer is that it is always "better" to be truthful because the prudential evasion derives from and continues to breed what Harvard Knowles and David Weber have called "sophisticated selfishness" — and that is the worst result of our moral miseducation. My second answer is that while one's integrity in telling the truth is vital, students and faculty should agree that dishonesty is less heinous than lack of charity. In the Knowles-Weber article the powerful antithesis of and antidote to "sophisticated selfishness" is "determined charity." When we first began thinking about planning the Summer Institute, I was sure that charity, as Saint Paul meant it, is the supreme virtue.

We must address ourselves to the important issue of the consequences of honesty for our students. But we must not, I believe, allow our moral concerns to be mainly secular. I suppose that if we believe that our schools are primarily in the business of producing academic excellence, then we are likely to decide that honesty is more important than caring for others. And we are likely to be puzzled, as one of my colleagues is, when I argue that in a hierarchy of student crimes "hazing," and not dishonesty, should head the list.

Our principal value should be a spiritual value. I am not talking about meekness, I am talking about love, or about what we often call caring. By extension, of course, I am also talking about dedication to service of our fellow man.

When Marty Bunting tells Abner Coates, "You need to get yourself organized. You ought to get married," he is implying a kind of connection that we can appropriate as an analogy to the didactic and the contextual approaches to moral education. These approaches are complementary, and I hope that none of us will say to himself — "Moral education is having the headmaster or the school minister give a serious talk, or it is a required course in ethics, but I don't see what it has to do with how faculty members perceive their work or why students are puzzled about sexuality." Conversely, I hope that none of us will say to himself — "Moral education is a matter of governance — students need responsibility for their lives and moral decisions, or it is a matter of creating a spirit of colleagueship in the faculty, but it is not hortatory exercises by various administrators and teachers who don't understand the mulish self-centeredness of adolescents."

The Summer Institute was successful in large part because Ted steered us in the right direction; and it sustained that successful beginning because imaginative and thoughtful participants like Chas Twichell seized on the value of a careful examination of the contextual approach to moral education. Chas' report on the Institute to his faculty is excellent.

But I dissent from one point in his report: he refers to a skepticism that the didactic approach to moral education works. Chas is right in his reading of the Institute. But I would urge us to consider the ending of the Knowles-Weber article carefully. "The students don't want us to be moral autocrats; they do want us to be moral advocates, of a sort." I read that statement amidst the surrounding ideas the authors present on the efficacy of faculty members, and in particular the headmaster, making public statements on moral principles. Stephen Kurtz did that superbly at Exeter this winter.

In a meeting of some students and faculty, he approached contextually the issue of why students "party" — but the force of his remarks were felt, by me at least, didactically. That is, he said what he believed ought to be happening in the moral education of students and of teachers. He took seriously one of the major pleas of the Institute: Leadership in moral education must come from the top. A scattering of alumni from the Institute cannot lead; but we can support those who do lead. I hope that the trustees and headmasters will speak out against the destructive kinds of competition in our schools, and that you will affirm that in spite of the secularity of most of our schools, that our primary values are spiritual ones. I think that's what down-to-earth Marty Bunting means when he urges Abner to get married. Commit yourself, he seems to say, to what is most precious. And then the rich contextual opportunities will be apparent to you every minute of the day.

XVIII

MORAL EDUCATION: AN ESSAY
Charles L. Terry

As John Phillips perceptively noted, teachers must be concerned with moral education as well as with the dispensation of knowledge. His admonition is imperative today for those charged with the education of adolescents; but few will agree on how best to combine goodness and knowledge. Lawrence Kohlberg, the most prominent thinker in this country on moral education, for the most part agrees with the Platonic assumption that goodness is the result of the compelling knowledge of principled conduct. And teachers, even some at Exeter, by and large seem to assume that questions of goodness are to be answered exclusively in the terms of knowledge.

John Phillips, on the other hand, was not a Platonist, for he did not assume that knowledge, even knowledge of goodness, compelled men to be moral. He was wise enough to discern that intellectual distinction can breed selfishness and cynicism; unaccompanied by a spirit of charity, unaccompanied by a dedication to service, knowledge can be "dangerous." Were he here today, he would argue that the Platonic formula is blind to the frequent disparity between judgment and action.

Most secondary schools do much better in knowledge than in goodness — particularly those engaged in the uncompromising pursuit of academic excellence. Instead of the link between knowledge and goodness that Phillips envisioned there is more likely to be, at best, a potentially creative tension between them. For a teacher of gifted students in a boarding school the experience of the classroom and the experience of the dormitory can be radically different ones; and often the fulfillment of the classroom can be a bewildering contrast to the frustration of the dormitory. It is possible, for example, to read an eloquent student essay on King Lear's discovery of charity and to see that same student act uncharitably toward other students in his dormitory.

The problem is, to a great extent, that students are inclined to see a disparity between what they call "academics" on the one hand and social development on the other. They are willing, nay eager, to grant a teacher authority in the classroom, but they often fiercely challenge that teacher's authority in their residential life. And even in the classroom they are not always willing to accept the teacher's authority in terms of values, except for the value of rigorous critical analysis. They recognize a teacher's authority in furnishing them with a method, a method, significantly, that enables them to experiment with ideas, and even in some academic disciplines to see ambiguity not only as tolerable, but perhaps desirable. Given this point of view, it is logical for them to expect that if our institutions are consistent, we will provide the same kind of opportunity for flexibility in the residential life of the school that we provide in the classroom.

In a way they are implicitly stating what people who have spent much time and thought on moral education have recently concluded. For a number of years Lawrence Kohlberg has favored a didactic scheme for moral education, based on classroom discussions of moral dilemmas. But recently he and others have been moving toward a contextual scheme — specifically the creation of a "just community" in schools, a "just community" because students themselves are given a major role in the governance of such a community.

But what if the faculty in a boarding school determines that such a democratic process is not sound education and that it is an inordinately time-consuming process? In that case a kind of full-fledged contextual education is not viable. Furthermore, what if students are reluctant to accept the responsibility for enforcing such rules or agreements as they themselves have had a significant role in establishing? In boarding schools these conditions frequently obtain, so that in fairness to their students and, moreover, in fairness to the parents of those students, faculties are wary of following Kohlberg's model of a "just community."

But faculties have been equally wary of what they often consider faddish classroom discussions and the exhortations of the didactic approach. We are in troubled waters for we are skeptical of both didactic moral education and of contextual moral education, which entitles students to have a major role in the governance of their community. Perhaps it is possible to blend the didactic and the contextual approaches in a way that will take advantage of the culture of our school.

What we need to look at are the implicit values of our community — the "hidden curriculum," if you will. Harvard Knowles and David Weber offer this analysis of these implicit values:

> ...all of us have known students who graduated from our schools with highly distinguished academic records but with minimal interest in other people, with imperceptible commitments to compassion or service. But most or all of us want to work in schools that try to nourish and that *tend* to nourish a less selfish orientation toward life; we want to create environments which encourage generosity of spirit and principled decision-making, not sophisticated selfishness, in our students and ourselves.[1]

In order to create such an environment we need to ask ourselves questions about the ethos of our institutions, and we need to make ourselves intentional moral educators — in both the didactic and contextual modes — and to help those of our colleagues reluctant to assume the role to become intentional moral educators.

What are our goals as such intentional moral educators? Knowles and Weber argue that caring for one another should be at the center of our life as a community. However, largely as a result of the atmosphere of ruthless academic competition in schools most likely to attract gifted students, self-seeking seems to the gifted, no matter how perceptive in other respects, the school's unofficial badge of attendance and even of graduation. How do we convince them that appearances to the contrary, this is not what our pride in academic achievement is supposed to produce?

Let us go back to the student who writes eloquently on King Lear's discovery of charity, but who leaves the classroom and returns to his dormitory demonstrating in his treatment of other students a distinct absence of charity. To this student such inconsistency is, as we have already remarked, defensible. However, it is also possible to see this student act uncharitably toward his classmates in the very class in which he wrote the essay. We might argue, then, that the first way to "form the minds and morals of the youth," in Phillips' phrase, is to enable them to see the reasonableness of transferring intellectual convictions to social ones in the classroom. Indeed, such transferring of learning to life can be the most exciting experience available to the young; and what more promising way to bring about a commerce of intellectual and social activity than that available in such a classroom atmosphere as in Exeter's Harkness system — a dozen students sitting around a table with their teacher, the students with guidance from the teacher, assuming the burden of the discussion. The system offers the ideal setting for a subtle combination of contextual and didactic moral education.

In such a context the students can begin to see that the success of the class depends as much, maybe even more, on its social chemistry, on its spirit of tolerance and openness, as it does on the ability of its members to think rapidly and to be highly verbal. If the teacher accedes to the radical wisdom in the statement "the 'subject matter' of the lesson [is] the responses of the learners to the questions they confront," then perhaps the students can begin to incorporate this attitude into their conviction of what is most fundamental in the process of learning.[2]

In becoming intentional moral educators, teachers and students have the rare opportunity of striving toward being a model of what an educated human being realizes: "The noblest character," to borrow Phillips' phrase, is one in which mind and heart are perfectly integrated, poised in a balance. In a recent book, *Promoting Moral Growth: From Piaget to Kohlberg*, the authors note that "Moral judgment is the area in which Piaget has dealt most explicitly with the relationship between cognition and affect"; and they go on to offer this definition: "For what is moral judgment if not a cognitive structuring of how we feel we ought to treat others and how others ought to treat us?"[3] It is this kind of passionate intelligence that students can encounter in the final awareness of Gabriel Conroy, the principal character in Joyce's greatest story, "The Dead." Conroy, an example of moral growth in fiction if ever there was one, thinks deeply because he feels deeply and vice versa. If such an experience is at the heart of moral education, then perhaps moral education is really what schools are most fundamentally about.

Even though gifted students are usually intent upon being independent of the teacher's values, it is possible to confront them with powerful moral ideas that form the thematic core of a course or part of it. Students can be made aware of the critical moral issues imbedded in what would otherwise be a routine set of assignments. In a course on chemistry, for example, the teacher can turn a unit on chemical reactions or acid or combustion into moral education by focusing attention on burning coal (carbon) and such impurities as sulphur. Students can be asked to discuss what goes up the smokestack besides carbon dioxide, water and soot. As soon as they learn that SO_2 dissolves to form a weak acid, they can quite naturally engage in a discussion of acid rain. Then the discussion can move along to the question of whether pollution control should be local or regional, where the jurisdictions no longer coincide with those that provide the political or legal power. By this time the class is discussing the broader issue of what to do when problems transcend our controlling social structures. The students are deeply involved as they begin to take a stand on conflicting answers to technical, social and ultimately moral questions.

It is difficult to teach American history without engaging students in moral issues. In dealing with the middle of the nineteenth century from the election of Andrew Jackson in 1828 to the end of Reconstruction in 1877 there is no better theme than the effect of racial attitudes on public and private policy. Instead of concentrating on the political conflicts between Jackson and John C. Calhoun and between Abraham Lincoln and Stephen A. Douglas, it can be more rewarding to ask students to consider the underlying influence of racial attitudes on these men and their actions. How do the students explain the paradox of Jackson's belief in democracy and his defense of slavery? Between Calhoun's insistence on liberty and his conviction that slavery should be the basis of Southern society? Ask students to decide whether they would have gone to war to destroy or defend the institution of slavery. Ask students to look at the issue of human rights through the eyes of Frederick Douglass or Jefferson Davis. And in dealing with Reconstruction ask the members of the class to decide how they would have dealt with the freedmen after the Civil War. Would they have cared more about human rights or sectional peace? The parallel between the moral issues in the 1860's and those in the 1960's will readily become apparent.[4]

An entire English course can be shaped around a moral issue. At Exeter, for example, one teacher has built a semester course for Seniors around the theme of charity as seen in *King Lear, Paradise Lost* and *The Brothers Karamazov*. At the start the students have been given as their first assignment Knowles and Weber's article on moral education. It is a useful assignment because the conclusions in the article are inductively based on instances of school life that are a part of the student's immediate experience. The assignment is also pedagogically sound because students get to become critics of two teachers' writing, and this offers a special kind of engagement for them: they see dedicated people trying to come to grips with the meaning of their professional work. Given the subject, "The Residential School as a Moral Environment," they also see those teachers' intense personal involvement in their profession.

It may be outrageously tendentious to open a course declaring that charity should be a major goal of the class for itself, and by extension for those students' larger involvement in the community, but when they realize that three works as diverse as *King Lear, Paradise Lost* and *The Brothers Karamazov* are vitally linked by the theme of love they get a glimpse of how great writers give "a cognitive structuring of how we feel we ought to treat others and how others ought to treat us." Lear's awareness of the inhumanity of rational attitudes toward existence which deny love and human responsibility for our fellow man is as indelible as Alyosha Karamazov's awareness of the truth of Father Zossima's dictum: "Hell is the inability to love." The brilliant tyrant of Hell, Milton's Satan, is, for students, reduced to eating ashes as the real drama of the poem becomes the simple heroism of two fallen human beings reconciling themselves to each other in unselfish love.

Gifted students must ultimately be purged of the cant that "academics" are mere methodology, or that "facts," as they sometimes disdainfully say, have nothing to do with one's social and emotional being. The classroom *is* the center of our schools, and we should affirm that idea boldly, at the same time redressing the balance in those classrooms so that intellect and emotion are as perfectly integrated as we can make them. And then, superb day, our classrooms will be the models for the larger community, and we will know when we pursue "excellence" just what we mean by that word.

---

1. *The Phillips Exeter Academy Bulletin*, November 1978, p. 15.
2. Neil Postman and Charles Weingartner, *Teaching As A Subversive Activity* (New York: Delacorte Press, 1969), p. 75.
3. Richard H. Hersh, Diana P. Paolitto, and Joseph Reimer, *Promoting Moral Growth: From Piaget to Kohlberg* (New York: Longman, 1979), p. 39.
4. I am grateful to Donald B. Cole for this paragraph on teaching American history and to C. Arthur Compton for the preceding paragraph on teaching chemistry.

XIX

EPILOGUE

His manly jowl is at war with his angelic look. He has played football at Exeter and Princeton; now his skills are theoretical: as he speaks to us, he breathes the ether of economics, telling us of "supply siding" and "monetarism." Behind him hangs an undistinguished curtain, not of Exeter red, but of deep blue; above the curtain are holes here and there in the window panes so feebly patched by World War II blackout paper that one of the patches flaps in the gusts from the October outside. We are addressing the incongruous and patchy world of stagflation, and, as Fitzgerald once said of an occasion far less sober, "The party has begun."

It is the formal opening of Exeter's protracted birthday party — the Bicentennial. After Bruce MacLaury has spoken of the economy, we will hear the mellifluous Gallic voice of Jean Mayer and then Edwin Reischauer, ailing, but superbly gathering his pedagogic and ambassadorial presences, will tell us of the state of the world. By the time we will have moved into the Assembly Hall almost twenty-four hours later, three distinguished panels will have concluded independently of each other that the most crucial transfusion for American education in the next twenty years must come, as Elizabeth Kennan of Mt. Holyoke states it, from teaching "self-discipline and compassion." All morning long there has been talk of "moral purpose," "goodness" and some panelists even have resorted to the phrase "moral education." Moral education is the overriding theme of the Bicentennial Symposium, October, 1980, just as it was the subject of Exeter's first Bicentennial Summer Institute, June, 1978. Do you catch John Phillips winking from that imposing portrait hanging in the Library?

About ten years ago Common Cause John Gardner said "passion without competence only adds to the confusion." We welcomed that wisdom because traditional academic knowledge and professionalism had come in the agonies of Vietnam and of our cities to be nearly dismissed by a large segment of the student population. We had to be "relevant," remember? Other voices, like Robert Brustein's, joined Gardner's and warned that "in order to be a doctor and help the sick of the ghettos, you must first study 'irrelevant' subjects like comparative anatomy and organic chemistry."

Of course, much of the "passion" of those days was insidiously selfish — what marched as commitment to something far beyond oneself too often swaggered into class as spiritual and moral arrogance so narcissistic that education nearly came to a standstill.

But in the decade since Gardner submitted his dictum we have lost the fire of the best passion of those days, the passion of categorical commitment to making ourselves better and the world a better place. A measure of that loss is manifest in the irony of the recent fashion of moral education: it was not Vietnam, but Watergate, that got us on the road to wondering how we could teach goodness. We still had Nixon to kick around; that was a more bearable kind of implicit self-criticism than facing John Fairbank's indictment of Americans as "killers."

But the panelists at the Bicentennial Symposium seemed to be willing to examine deeper roots of sin than those of Watergate. One heard an urgent call for compassion and understanding that reverberates more substantially than a call for integrity. Perhaps the community of that Symposium was even persuaded that compassion will ultimately guarantee integrity and the pursuit of justice.

This book has argued the urgency of redressing the balance between passion and competence, between empathy and intelligence, between goodness and knowledge. Such a profoundly Christian word, passion, is of course religiously, as etymologically, linked with suffering, enduring. But as Shakespeare's Hamlet and Eliot's Becket so brilliantly mingled enduring *with* acting, so we can think of passion as both empathizing with our fellow man and acting responsibly on the insights of that empathy in order to put our vast intellectual achievements to work for the good of community, nation and the world.

II

We are a rather sparse gathering — we hardly fill half of the Elting Room at Exeter, the room where the faculty meets each week. We are here today to hear Phillip W. Turner, Professor of Ethics at

General Theological Seminary, address the subjects "The Substance of Modern Ethics" and "The Teaching of Ethics." "We" are about forty-five clergymen and teachers of religion attending a two-day Bicentennial Conference on "Ethics and the Problem of Evil." The evening before we have heard Elie Wiesel speak on that subject and declare that "knowledge without ethics is evil": Exeter students who heard Wiesel are not likely ever to forget that moment.

Turner will tell us that we teachers must be models for our students, that we must stand for something, not simply be "value-free facilitators" of a classroom discussion. Douglas Heath has told the Summer Institute the same thing two years ago, and as Exeter harvests the richness of this Bicentennial emphasis on moral purpose, we are renewed in our awareness that a teacher ought to stand for values, and that if he or she is lucky, those values and the values of the school can be commensurate with one another, or at least complementary. A teacher should reflect the core of belief in values as do people like Frederick Buechner — former School Minister at Exeter, who preached the sermon of rededication at the October Bicentennial Symposium; people like Joseph Reimer, friend of Exeter as well as resource colleague at the Summer Institute on Moral Education. Joseph Reimer has preached twice at Phillips Church, bearing witness to the meaning of goodness in human life. For some he has, in his brilliant capacity to preach in the Rabbinical tradition, prepared the way for Elie Wiesel, the man who spoke from the authority of his experience: "...knowledge without ethics is evil."

Christopher Brookfield suggested to a plenary session of the Summer Institute on Moral Education that good ideas such as those he knew were emerging from the Institute would probably take at least three years to become viable in our schools. What an accurate prophet he was: Exeter has been extraordinarily blessed in its Bicentennial year with individual gifts of precious jewels that can be gathered into a stunning crown. The plea from Reischauer to be compassionate and understanding in our attitude toward people of other lands; the sensible observation in the Bicentennial Symposium panel discussions of Arthur Powell of the Commission on Educational Issues to seek the answer to "whither education in these next twenty years?" in moral purpose; the passionate statements from another panelist, John Ratté of Loomis Chaffee, to the same point; the sermon of Frederick Buechner apprising us of the sacredness of *all* human experience; the reiteration of that theme in Elie Wiesel's telling boys and girls—"my friends" he called them—that when they hurt another human being they deny God.

When this abundance of grace is made available to a community, it is difficult to imagine it being resisted. But we know history, so what can we say to the skeptics, who, nevertheless, bring good will to their consideration of such claims for moral education, to their consideration of the proposition that "knowledge without goodness is dangerous"?

III

The late Henry Bragdon, teacher of history at Exeter, said the Academy's task was obvious: we get good boys and girls, and we teach them skills that will make them effective citizens. And even though Henry wrote to his friend McGeorge Bundy in the 60's deploring our war in Vietnam, he did not always absorb the profound irony in the phrase "the best and the brightest." So fundamentally optimistic was his nature and disposition that he did not fully perceive what Douglas Heath and Phillip Turner identify as a new hedonism, a privatism that looks on morals nowadays as largely, in Turner's words, "a matter of style." We have our own "lifestyles"; we speak of "my orientation."

If we ask "Academic excellence for what?" Turner answers sadly that the current fashion is "to maximize our material and psychic portfolios." It is so true, and it is especially painful to think of how teachers who have preached academic excellence to the exclusion of other concerns have been used by the forces of materialism and hedonism. Those academicians must have held up, and continue to hold up, the value of the life of the mind. But academic excellence has been forged, while we were not looking, into an instrument of selfishness.

The charming girl speaking at the student panel for the Conference on Ethics and the Problem of Evil says that her primary ethical concern is to "develop a self"; she cannot address herself to moral dilemmas unless she has a "self" capable of adjudicating between choices. Her earnestness is so winning, and yet she does not perceive the irony in her route to autonomy. She represents the "atomic individual" Turner has been talking about; she does not realize that for figures as diverse as Augustine and Thoreau the self gets defined by commitment to something outside one's psyche. Turner reminds us that for Plato and Aristotle being a citizen is a necessary condition for developing the self; that for Augustine discipleship enables one to develop the self. This girl is perpetuating the modern fallacy that somehow morality is a completely private matter, a matter really of intimacy, not of public responsibility, and despite the very probable strength of this girl's capacity to deal with intimacy, many of her generation have been bewildered by the task of coping with it.

IV

Exeter's proposal for a summer institute on moral education bore the title "Can Our Schools Teach Personal Morality?" We quickly learned from those who have thought long and hard about the subject that schools are, willy-nilly, moral teachers. Sometimes of course the education is, unfortunately, miseducation, but moral education goes on irrespective of intention. But "personal morality" — what did we mean by that? Were we thinking of developing autonomous moral agents like the charming panelist, or were we thinking of making traditional values so compelling that our students would adopt them? Perhaps we wanted it, and continue to want it, both ways.

Henry Bragdon cast a skeptical eye on the whole enterprise. Nevertheless, he was both an autonomous self and an altruistic spirit. He once praised Erich Fromm's *The Art of Loving* as a book defining the absolute core of effective human endeavor. He was a man with a strong sense of self and a great capacity for love.

Isn't that the model we want for our students? That is the kind of model that John Pittenger, Exeter 1947, and John Irving, Exeter 1961, cherished more than anything else in their experience in school. Pittenger might say, if asked "Academic excellence for what?" — in order to become a human being like Henry Bragdon, a human being far richer than Henry's own notion of an effective citizen, a human being capable of loving, of extending charity wherever he was. And for John Irving the model was Ted Seabrooke, another man with a strong sense of self and a great capacity for love. Pittenger and Irving, distinguished graduates of Exeter, have made obvious the power of the life of the mind. They would probably credit this school for heading them toward that fullfillment. But their eloquence in eulogizing their teachers attests finally to character, to goodness, to love. Cultivating the life of the mind enables us to live the life of the spirit. In the end, it is the life of the spirit that Henry Bragdon and Ted Seabrooke exemplified, and because they exemplified that life, they endure.

We must teach "self-discipline and compassion." In order to help us do that we must be willing to examine our lives and our institutions, we must be willing to reflect upon our goals, we must be ardently in search of a vision of education that integrates knowledge and goodness.

APPENDIX A

A Talk in Phillips Church, May, 1977
Thomas W. Holcombe
(formerly of Exeter, now of Kent School)

Scripture from Romans, 12:1-2

I have at various times in the past been critical of speeches given from this pulpit at the Thursday services because though they have often been very stimulating, they seemed more like lectures than sermons. I hope you will forgive me for making a hypocrite of myself by following their example on this one last occasion I shall have to speak in this place. You will have to judge for yourself whether what I will say is God's truth or merely my personal opinion. I cannot claim I have always been clear as to the difference, and sometimes when I've wanted to imagine myself as a prophet I may have merely succeeded in playing the crank. The verdict is yours.

I'd like to share with you my thoughts on some of the ways in which a secular academic institution like Exeter influences the religious life of those within it. I'd like *not* to talk of the positive things — the attractive church building it provides, with all its facilities, its extraordinarily stimulating academic environment, and most of all, the remarkably talented people of all ages who make this school what it is. I think we at Exeter pat ourselves on the back quite enough.

Instead I'd like to talk about some of the *negative* things which make authentic ministry in such a place extraordinarily difficult, which have given me personally such a strong sense of frustration and failure. We who attempt to minister here are subject to a set of unspecified yet nonetheless binding role expectations which it is nearly impossible for any fallible human being to fulfill. But I'm not even going to talk about those.

Because the problem is intrinsic to the academic institution itself. As is so often the case, its great strength is from another point of view, a debilitating weakness. Its secularism represents its freedom from ecclesiastical domination, a freedom which an ever-increasing portion of the faculty and administration have been arduously seeking and jealously guarding. Freedom is a good thing. It enables the school to attract a broad diversity of students and faculty, the value of which no one calls into question. And pluralism is a good thing.

But the spiritual person at some point becomes keenly aware of something missing which he feels is especially important. What he misses in the secular academic institution is the sense of its rootedness in the common ground of being, the source of life which is none other than God himself. Thus the institution can never be identified with the community of faith, to which he owes his primary allegiance if he is really a spiritual person. And so the community of faith must hack out a clearing for itself in the midst of the institutional woods, without being able to count on the greater institution to expedite the process. In fact, it may actually hinder it. And who is going to hack out this clearing? Is there a strong religious community to start with, an *ecclesia* constituted by the shared commitment of its members to a common world-view, a lifestyle of mutual love and service, in short, a *faith?* In such a pluralistic environment there is *not.* If there *is* to be a congregation we have to *create* one, and it is an extremely difficult task.

If faith is not the cohesive factor integrating this school, as John Phillips intended it to be so many years ago, then what *is?*

To the extent to which this institution is an integrated community at all, it is so on a radically secular basis. In fact, since the abolition of compulsory chapel attendance this school's common institutional life can no longer be said to have any religious dimension at all. It is rather the classroom, its extensions the library and the dormitory room, and the playing field which determine the character of our common life. Interestingly, these are all places where a sense of competition is consciously or unconsciously stimulated. The church is the one place where the principle of competition is rigorously excluded, and as such it finds itself somewhat at odds with the ethos of the greater academic community in which it is set.

Then how do we in the church achieve that sense of religious community, which we consider to be so very essential, when such a community doesn't exist to begin with?

We use a number of stratagems. Intellectually, we try to convince people of the common, shared quality of their humanness, and the need for them to encounter each other at this level. The need for them to build each other up, not tear each other down. Individualism has gotten a little out of hand in our culture.

Then we try to define the church as the locus where this sort of deep interpersonal encounter takes place. We attempt to provide people with a shared experience of worship, of different types of events which they can participate in and react to as a *group* instead of as individuals only.

One of the less subtle ways in which we attempt to create a sense of community is our arrangement of the seating — this distinctive diamond pattern of the pews. Instead of looking at the backs of others in front of us, the way we do in most churches, here we gather around a common center facing each other across the middle. Instant community!

Yet what do we place *in* this center in our midst? Some churches have a void there. We have a table — not an altar, to be sure, but at least a table. With plants or flowers beautifully arranged on it, which are very nice. But what we *lack* is an integrating symbol at this focal point of our community — for Christians, the cross, and perhaps the bread and wine, or the scriptures; for Jews, perhaps the ark containing the scrolls of the Torah. We have good motives for omitting these symbols here: we are in a pluralistic setting and would not give offense to any of different persuasion.

But these symbols have tremendous cohesive power in our two great religious traditions, and when we deny them we lose that which has integrated our communities of faith all down through the ages. The lack of a symbol here indicates that in our pluralism we cannot agree on the meaning of our center, which suggests just how superficial our sense of community here really is.

Our introverted seating arrangement suggests another difficulty we have in our religious life within the greater academy context. We are very much preoccupied with *ourselves* and with our own growth. We ministers have perhaps rather uncritically brought the concern of the classroom into the church as well; it *is* habit-forming. Yet Jesus would have us temper this self-centeredness: "Seek ye first the kingdom of God, and these things will be added unto you." "Deny yourself, and take up your cross...." True growth comes when you focus not on yourself, but on others around you and on your heavenly Lord.

Outside the church there are even more subtle difficulties which beset us. I say this because the academic institution founds its self-understanding on two postulates which the spiritual person has to reject as erroneous.

The first of these two postulates is what I would call the "objectivist" fallacy, one that has been very prevalent in higher education in our lifetime. It has become fashionable in many circles to define "truth" as something "out there," which can be properly known only when the subjective human variable is eliminated as a relevant factor. Accordingly, truth becomes externalized, objectified and inert, a thing which may interest us intellectually, but which may not have any deeper meaning for us. The question of personal meaning is not allowed because it assumes the importance of the subjective factor for truth.

This fallacy the great psychologist Carl Gustav Jung protested vigorously. He argued that a person merely by willing it cannot eliminate himself as a variable in the process of perception because perception is conditioned by whatever areas of bias and selective inattention the perceiver may have. His mind conditions what he looks for and identifies as significant and allows as truth.

The spiritual person must be prepared to go even further. He has an intuitive grasp of truth and a sense of relatedness to it, which other people may not share. He then must protest that truth is not a static objective thing "out there" somewhere waiting to be empirically observed. Rather, it is a dynamic all-encompassing reality in which we participate, which includes us all as total human beings, and with which we may feel a sense of relatedness. In this all-encompassing truth, human subjectivity is essential, because that is where truth lives itself out in us. This truth, of course, is God himself, in whom we live and move and have our being. And in us he lives and moves and has his being. We are inextricable.

The second postulate of the academic institution which the spiritual person must protest is what I would call the "teleological" fallacy. It has to do with the self-defined educational goals of the school, which determine (or rather, reflect) its established character. I could put this differently by saying the institution defines the human problem in terms with which it is both inclined — and best suited — to deal. Whether its special competence arises from its inclination toward a certain model of education, or vice versa, I would hesitate to say. The fact remains, however, that most of our finest schools nowadays see the human problem in terms of ignorance and incompetence. They can deal with these because they are highly effective at conveying information and teaching manipulative skills, both mental and physical. If you examine the ways in which the publicly stated goals of Exeter have changed over the last two centuries you will quickly see how this institution, like so many others, has zeroed in on ignorance and incompetence.

The spiritual person, however, is very sensitive to what has been lost in these two hundred years, for it is precisely the religious dimension of life which has been defined out of common concern; the religious vision — which so distinguished John Phillips — has been lost. The authentically religious concern is *not* primarily the acquisition of knowledge, as useful as knowledge is to all of us. Those living in the time of the early Christian church who felt it was were condemned by the church fathers as gnostics and heretics. St. Paul, for instance, wrote, "knowledge *puffs* us, but love *builds* up." Jesus himself attacked the great teachers of his day, the Pharisees, for their self-inflation and distortion of the truth.

Nor is the authentically religious concern primarily for the acquisition of competencies either. If *only* the intelligent and knowledgeable and skilled are able to enter the Kingdom, then *God help* the poor, the lonely and the outcast.

But in truth the spiritual person must insist that the human problem lies somewhere else. It is the problem of rich and poor, of the able and the not-so-able alike, regardless of their degree of intelligence or education. It cuts across the lines separating "all sorts and conditions of men," and women. It is *not* ignorance and incompetence, but something much more difficult to conceptualize and deal with. It is the problem of estrangement and alienation, which in centuries past has been called the problem of *sin*.

Our estrangement from God — that is the point of the doctrine of the Fall — and our estrangement from each other. Perhaps there is a correlation between the two. And even more, as we have learned from psychology in the last fifty years, estrangement from ourselves. We must insist that this brokenness, or *sin*, and *not ignorance*, is the crux of the human problem. The wages of ignorance are mediocrity, but the wages of *sin* are *death*.

So we who attempt to be ministers in an academic institution like Exeter are faced with many difficulties. Like Socrates we are called to be "gadflies on the rump of Athens" — the cradle of democracy, drama, philosophy, the intellectual quest. It is a dangerous business because the situation is one in which our spiritual integrity is so easily co-opted and compromised. We are accountable to those who do not necessarily share our faith, our values, our vocation. If we are gadflies, our vocation is to sting the beast on which we find ourselves, prodding it out of its self-satisfied complacency, reminding it that it must always keep moving toward greener pastures. But if we sting it too hard it flicks us off with a sweep of its tail and thrusts us out into thin air. As St. Paul once wrote, "We have become, and are now, as the refuse of the world, the offscouring of all things." Amen.

APPENDIX B

Can Our Schools Teach Personal Morality?

A Proposal for a Summer Institute for Teachers

Submitted by
PHILLIPS EXETER ACADEMY
EXETER, NEW HAMPSHIRE

INTRODUCTION

Phillips Exeter Academy was founded in response to the two major spiritual movements of the eighteenth century — the American Revolution and the religious awakenings which both preceded and followed it. In the deed of gift by which he established an academy in the town of Exeter, John Phillips, active churchman and member of the local Revolutionary committee of correspondence, emphasized that a free republic requires educated citizens who value service to mankind more than self-serving. He insisted that it must be the primary duty of the instructors in his academy to look to the moral and spiritual development of their students and that "knowledge without goodness is dangerous." He also required that the Academy must be open to talented scholars regardless of their economic circumstances, and he left his ample fortune and lands that these ends might be met.

In preparation for the observance of the Bicentennial of the Academy's founding in 1781 the faculty and trustees have decided to examine the meaning of educational excellence — to explore what modern society demands in the training of its educated leaders, to share with teachers from public secondary schools and other independent schools those methods of teaching which have outstanding results at Exeter, and to join with others in the search for answers to problems which have produced a sense of crisis about contemporary secondary education.

We propose to act as host for a series of summer institutes for teachers from June 1978 through June 1981, the period marking our bicentennial celebration. Themes which we recognize to be of critical importance are the teaching of morality, the decline of written expression, advances in the teaching of mathematics and the natural sciences, and literature and the challenge of relevance.

We seek financial support for a 1978 summer institute which is to explore the teaching of morality and the communication of values. Much attention has been given recently to the proposition that morality can be taught as a separate subject in the curriculum. We wish to examine this thesis carefully, to learn what the results of several experimental courses at other institutions have been, and to consider what the strengths and weaknesses of traditional approaches appear to be.

STATEMENT OF THE PROBLEM

In an article entitled "Moral Education" which appeared in the March 1, 1976 issue of *Newsweek* the statement is made that "there is now a sense of urgency in this country for moral education comparable to the urgency felt for scientific education in the late fifties following Sputnik." The authors of the article point out that the most prominent educator in the field today, Professor Lawrence Kohlberg of the Harvard Center for Moral Development and Education, bases his theory of the moral education of students according to rational discourse on the Platonic belief that knowledge about what is just should compel virtuous behavior.

At Phillips Exeter Academy the cognitive tradition in education has always been dominant. After visiting the Academy in October 1976 the evaluation committee of the Commission on Secondary Schools of the New England Association of Schools and Colleges observed "a strong tendency for some faculty to assume that knowledge and goodness were almost completely interchangeable concepts and to restate any question about 'goodness' as though it were a question about 'knowledge'."

Aside from courses in ethics under the aegis of the Academy's Department of Religion there is no attempt to teach moral decision-making and moral behavior in a systematic way. The ethos of the Academy implies that, like knowledge, goodness is teachable, yet the faculty does not attempt to teach its students in any formal manner about making moral decisions and acting according to them.

A wise and distinguished retired teacher of history at the Academy argues that the point of our efforts is to take good people and to teach them skills that will enable them to become effective citizens. As persuasively as he makes the point, some of us consider that this formula is no longer acceptable. Even if our students arrive as "good people" (and this assumption is surely debatable), they quickly enter what William V. Shannon of the New York *Times* has described as "the enemy territory" of youth culture where postponement of personal gratification becomes the mark, not of maturity, but of immaturity. At Exeter, it might be remarked parenthetically, students' refusal to postpone gratification often leads to the kinds of deception and dishonesty that break down trust between adults and adolescents. We are not only failing to prepare our students for moral behavior in the world, we are failing to realize a precious sense of relatedness within the community of the school itself.

The formula of taking "good people" and teaching them skills to make them effective citizens has been challenged by a young teacher of religion at Exeter:

> The institution defines the human problem in terms with which it is both inclined and best suited to deal. Whether its special competence arises from its inclination toward a certain model of education, or vice versa, I would hesitate to say. The fact remains, however, that most of our finest schools nowadays see the human problem in terms of ignorance or incompetence. They can deal with these, because they are highly effective at conveying information and teaching manipulative skills, both mental and physical. If you examine the ways in which the publicly stated goals of Exeter have changed over the last two centuries you will quickly see how this institution, like so many others, has zeroed in on ignorance and incompetence.... But in truth, the spiritual person must insist that the human problem lies somewhere else. It cuts across lines separating all sorts and conditions of men and women. It is not ignorance and incompetence, but something more difficult to conceptualize and deal with. It is the problem of estrangement and alienation, which in centuries past has been called the problem of sin.... We must insist that that brokenness, or *sin*, and *not ignorance*, is the crux of the human problem. The wages of ignorance are mediocrity, but the wages of *sin* are *death*.

Obviously, the points of view of the retired history teacher and of the young teacher of religion are radically opposite, but one should not automatically assume that there is no possibility of accommodation between them. In a recent Academy catalogue — that of September 1975 — there appears under the title "Goals of Exeter" the assertion that "the creative link between goodness and knowledge has been, and remains, Exeter's central purpose." That statement defines a sound and noble educational desideratum, and it would be eminently worthwhile to give serious study to how that creative link can be forged.

PROPOSAL FOR STUDYING THE PROBLEM

We propose a summer institute to be held at Phillips Exeter Academy in July 1978 that will seek answers to the following questions: Is "goodness" best taught in academic courses? What model or models of such teaching provide the best results? (The Taft School, for example, has what it describes as "an evolving program," a program now three years old, which requires tenth-grade students to take a term course in which they discuss questions on the conduct of their lives mainly at school, questions dealing with drugs, stealing, cheating and sexual behavior. The Council for Religion in Independent Schools of New Haven, Connecticut, has for a number of years been encouraging instructors of religion to incorporate discussion of these moral problems in their courses by distributing case studies to them.) How can the environment of a boarding school offer means beyond the cognitive approach of the classroom to inculcate morality in its students? How effective is the religious ethos of a school in guiding students to moral decision-making and moral actions?

We do not see that we can consider questions of moral education in an exclusively secular context. We are also aware of the apparent bond between educators like Kohlberg and educators who also happen to be school ministers or chaplains and teachers of religion. We are vitally interested in the commerce of ideas between the secular and the religious advocates of moral education.

We propose a three-part program: first, an initial period of identifying the basic philosophical issues, such as, What is the end of moral education?; second, the major period of time devoted to seeking answers to the questions we have posed for study; and third, a period of reflection, and in particular, serious reflection on the complementarity of secular and religious approaches to the problems we have defined.

We expect that this reflection may well lead to useful publication.

Leaders and resource persons would be drawn from school ministers, college and university teachers who have designed broad undergraduate courses in the humanities, and scholars of note in the field of the psychology of learning. We anticipate that the four or five resource persons would not be in residence for the entire length of the Institute and that their participation would be staggered with overlap to provide continuity. We believe that Professor Kohlberg should be invited to participate, and we have already made tentative plans with the Headmaster of Phillips Academy, Theodore R. Sizer, former Dean of the Harvard Graduate School of Education, to take part.

Twenty participants would be drawn primarily from secondary schools across the nation. Those interested in participating would be asked to submit a short essay defining their interest and possible contributions to the discussions. Prospective participants would be notified of their acceptance by February 1, 1978. They would be housed in Academy dormitories and fed in its dining hall.

CONCLUSION

In setting forth the subject of this proposal, and especially in suggesting the distinctive area of its pursuit, Exeter realizes that it is calling into question its most cherished heritage: academic excellence attained, if necessary, at the exclusion of other educational goals. Such a challenge seems appropriate for an honest self-examination on the occasion of the Academy's Bicentennial. We believe these summer institutes offer an opportunity for sharing the important things a distinguished school can do. Our intent is to encourage an exchange of ideas and to reduce the insularity of all who participate. Exeter will make a major contribution to the program in people, resources, and administrative energy, but it will also benefit greatly from the planning and the results.

APPENDIX C
Participants In The Summer Institute on Moral Education
June 18 - June 30, 1978

ANDOVER:
Vincent B. J. Avery
Albert K. Roehrig
Nathaniel B. Smith

CHOATE-ROSEMARY HALL:
Eleanore Drury
Arthur F. Goodearl, Jr.
Charles P. Twichell

DEERFIELD:
John Anderson
*Judd H. Blain
Parnell P. Hagerman

EXETER:
Charles A. Hamblet
Susan K. Jorgensen
Harvard V. Knowles

HOTCHKISS:
Stephen T. Bolmer
L. Timothy Doty
Blanche B. Hoar

LAWRENCEVILLE:
W. Graham Cole, Jr.
Marty Doggett
Samuel Harding

ST. PAUL'S:
Alden B. Flanders
Thomas J. Quirk, Jr.
Theodore Yardley

*Judd H. Blain was unable to attend.

It should also be noted that David R. Weber, an observer in the first week, stayed on as a participant throughout the remainder of the Institute.

Resource Colleagues of The Institute

Christopher M. Brookfield, *Dean of the Church Schools of Virginia*
Douglas Heath, *Professor of Psychology, Haverford College*
Robert Kegan, *Bureau of Study Counsel, Harvard University*
Lawrence Kohlberg, *Professor of Psychology and Director of The Center for Moral Education, Harvard Graduate School of Education*
Joseph Reimer, *Associate Professor, School of Education, Boston University*
Theodore R. Sizer, *Headmaster, Phillips Academy, Andover*
David R. Weber, *Instructor in English, Phillips Exeter Academy*

Directors of the Institute

Charles L. Terry, *Instructor in English, Phillips Exeter Academy*
Joseph E. Fellows, *Counselor, Phillips Exeter Academy*

APPENDIX D

Memorandum to President Charles Dey and the Choate-Rosemary Hall Community
Charles P. Twichell
I. Report on The Exeter Institute

INTRODUCTION

In the charters of both Andover and Exeter, the founders charged both schools to develop the minds and characters of students. The following pages record the participation and recommendations of Ellie Drury, Art Goodearl, and Chas Twichell, representatives to the conference from Choate-Rosemary Hall.

DEFINITIONS

Heaviest of heavy terms, "moral education" suggests the Puritans, Boy Scouts, daily chapel services, and a host of classical and modern philosophers and developmental psychologists. The members of the Insitute *labored* under the phrase. A looser definition or term might be "character education," or some catch phrase involving maturity that would keep the developmental psychologists happy. For the CRH delegation, "character education" will do better than moral education, though the phrases will be used interchangeably in these pages.

At our first meeting, Ted Sizer of Andover defined M.E. as "the development by deliberate means of principled behavior"; fundamental elements of morality were, said he, "fairness, compassion, commitment to service." It is certainly true that all of the seven schools present include in their stated aims a deep commitment to develop graduates with more than academic skills. CRH, for example, includes these objectives in its statement of purpose: (from our self-examination for the NEASC).

> ...to help students understand and become engaged in fundamental ethical and moral issues,
> ...to help students develop self-confidence, self-motivation, a sense of worth; to help them identify personal goals,
> ...to teach sportsmanship,
> ...to (encourage) a sense of humor,
> ...to foster greater respect for one's neighbor and greater appreciation for the interdependency of individuals within a community.

But how much time and effort do we and the other schools actually devote on a straight-line basis to achieve these goals? A good question! For years our daily chapel services at least pretended to nourish the moral being. But no school represented at the Institute felt that required chapel gave good results. In characterizing themselves, several schools spoke of the "aggressive, ruthless competition among students" for college admission. Students were termed "uncaring." Some schools spoke of coldly intellectual faculties who were too often in states of physical, emotional, or marital exhaustion themselves to devote their best thought and energy to teaching "goodness."

Let Moral Education be called character education, goodness and maturity training, or any other phrase; it was clear that the schools were taking few deliberate steps to encourage it.

PARTICIPANTS
Seven schools (Andover, Exeter, Deerfield, Hotchkiss, Lawrenceville, St. Paul's and CRH) sent three members each to the institute. Included were five deans, five chaplains or religious teachers, four counselors, historians, artists, mathematics, and English teachers. We were told that *we* were the experts, that we were expected not only to take back to our schools specific programs for implementation, but also to put enough of our ideas into print so that Exeter could publish a monograph of national significance as part of its 200th Anniversary in 1981. On both charges, a majority of delegates expressed great uneasiness.

OUTSIDE SPEAKERS
Guest speakers or consultants included Lawrence Kohlberg, noted Harvard Graduate School of Education developmental psychologist; his two able and articulate lieutenants, Joe Reimer and Bob Kegan; and the ubiquitous Douglas Heath of Haverford, a former CRH trustee, who was as spell-binding as ever.

CONFERENCE FORMAT
A brief description of the format of the conference may be helpful. There were three representatives from each of the seven schools. We assembled in full session or divided into three groups of seven to address agenda set before us by Exeter staff directing the Institute. The agenda was not confining, and I suspect the loose reins were intended to encourage digression, speculation, ventilation and fellowship. I found the delegates taking the whole business very seriously and working very hard to come to grips with the rather shapeless monster called Moral Education.

Within the twenty-one delegates were priests and pragmatists, talkers and listeners, deans, doctors, and astronauts. I flew in at the litter level, as you know, but more often we circled in the substratosphere of "human relations talk" where I found the oxygen a little thin.

On the first Monday each school gave a half-hour presentation to the whole group of its own scene, its problems and blueprints (if any) for their solution. A number of taped interviews with students gave interesting insights into the different schools and their very common problems. Early in the second week each school offered a fifteen-minute summary of what it thought it was doing right. (A listing and a brief description of some of the brighter ideas appears later.) On the next to the last day each school made its third formal presentation, this time setting forth the specific game plan its delegation hoped to implement during the upcoming school years.

From the three series of formal declarations and from the many hours of less structured discussion in smaller groups there emerged at least five very clear areas in which schools had encountered common problems. Each deserves discussion.

I. Discipline Systems and their Effectiveness

II. Faculty Role Models

III. The Need for Democratic Participation

IV. Contextual and Didactic Approaches

V. Competition as a Primary Enemy of Moral Education

ONE: Discipline Systems and their Effectiveness

Discipline systems are the easily visible apparatus of Character Education. They distinguish between good and bad, yes and no. CRH's system seems as good as any, better than some. Concentration of disciplinary power in a single person's hands can be a serious error, resented by students and faculty, who rightly demand sympathy and consistency and whose M.E. is greatly furthered by active participation.

The posture of the several schools toward the current bogeymen of drugs and drinks runs from stern (no second chance) to wishy-washy ("What's good for this student?") with CRH's "doctrine of the second chance" a majority stance. Most significant to me was the rather general agreement that disciplinary systems don't teach morality. Students don't necessarily feel guilty when caught and pledge sincerely to lead better lives; they feel stupid when caught and pledge to act smarter next time. Too rarely were schools able to impress upon students in disciplinary situations the moral implications and consequences to themselves and others of their actions.

TWO: Faculty Role Models

Role models *do* have an important impact upon students, particularly where individuals are willing to articulate clearly their own beliefs and values. All schools admitted having some less-than-perfect models on their staffs, particularly persons so preoccupied with their own jobs and activity as to be unlistening, insensitive, uncaring with students, even with each other. Any effort to improve the quality of faculty role models through any and all means is the best way to further the cause of M.E.

The means and methods of improving faculty role models is clearly a matter of vast size and infinite complexity. I have more doubt than confidence that we or any school can quickly, perhaps ever, create a host of saints and heroes from the cast of hardworking characters we have and know so well. But to improve the quality of life for faculty, to free faculty members from some of the anxieties and hardships they suffer, to give them the margins of time and privacy to be more than schoolmasters will directly strengthen them as role models and increase their already major role in the M.E. of our students.

THREE: The Need for Democratic Participation

M.E. is greatly enhanced by signficant student and faculty participation in as many areas of governance as possible. Though a school cannot be a pure democracy, it must force upon its citizens the need to debate and decide moral issues.

Unhappiest of all at the Exeter Conference were those from schools where tradition was heaviest, where autocratic concentration of power relieved too many others of any responsibility, where structured subdivisions created ironclad little worlds at the expense of flexibility and willingness to change.

In this area, CRH's past struggles toward becoming a single community have been a godsend. Because of them we seem remarkably free of any fear of change. M.E. requires a willingness to change, and the decision-making process must be widely shared.

FOUR: Contextual and Didactic Approaches

In his remarks at our first meeting, Ted Sizer distinguished between didactic (classroom courses, chapel talks) and contextual (experiential) education, concluding that since the "street" in a young person's life plays a vastly more influential educational role than the classroom, we must devise contextual rather than didactic means to further M.E. in our schools. As residential schools we clearly have opportunities day schools lack.

By the end of the ten days of groping for practicable ways to offer student bodies through dormitory and extracurricular activities enough contextual opportunities for M.E., the delegates were relieved and reassured to hear both Larry Kohlberg and Douglas Heath speaking more optimistically about what can be done in the classroom. Said they (paraphrased), "Your staffs are teachers, teaching is what they do best. One must use one's strengths." They then proceeded to show us how classes in any subject can be conducted to teach not only subject but, more important, to encourage such moral objectives as cooperation, tolerance, humor, patience and self-confidence. As one of the delegates put it, "There are ways to get more out of a math class than just geometry."

Required courses in religion, ethics, decision-making abound; mandatory chapel services are nearly extinct. No one at the Institute expressed real confidence that either scheme successfully made much of a mark on uninitiated students. The boy or girl already deeply interested in ethical or moral questions, or profoundly committed to a religious faith, will prosper in chapel or ethics class. We should not drop our course offerings or abandon efforts to provide a variety of spiritual/religious services in several dimensions for several denominations, but we must not expect them to achieve by themselves the kind of moral education we want.

FIVE: Competition as a Primary Enemy of Moral Education
The intensity with which schools like ours encourage and pursue academic excellence constitutes a major threat to the kind of atmosphere most conductive to moral education. Competition for grades, for places on teams, for college acceptance stresses the individual's skills, growth, achievement contrasted to those of others, his surpassing others rather than his helping others, even his identifying himself with others in joint enterprise. Too often it stresses the single person, too rarely the community; it emphasizes the functions of mind, thought and knowledge rather than those of heart, feelings and faith. One of its great weapons is the "put down." We have all seen countless incidents of students putting down one another; we see faculty putting down students; we see faculty in one department putting down those in another department, or even that whole field of study, as less important than their own.

If we accept fairness, compassion and a commitment to service as three attributes of the kind of morality we are seeking to teach, should we not be alarmed at the cruelty of the "put down"? Does the greater intensity of the competition in academic endeavors make less possible the opportunity for sound moral education? Are the two, in fact, mutually exclusive?

Preliminary Response and Some Heath Data

The response of the CRH delegation to the rhetorical question above is clearly negative. Academic and character education can be complementary; academic excellence need never threaten value education. In fact, some of Dr. Heath's researches suggest that only if sound character education precedes the academic will the latter have any lasting positive meaning the lives of college graduates.

II. Moral Education At CRH

Moral Education at CRH Now: Positive Side

The CRH delegation to Exeter took considerable pride in the number of ways we seemed to lead our fellow schools in M.E. already in operation. A brief comment upon the various opportunities will suffice.

1. Our *decision-making process,* including the limited override, involves so many students in so many ways that it offers real contextual opportunities for M.E. Student and faculty representation on Trustee Committees is a plus, as are all the others: Academic Committee, Judicial Committees, Student Council, Activities Committee, Mini-Term, House Counselors, CREC, and a dozen others.

2. *School Service Program,* involving all faculty and all students in a cooperative, non-competitive program of shared effort for the common welfare, is unique (so far) and absolutely the best kind of activity a school community can offer. Collaboration in non-academic chores, some of them unpleasant, is a valuable goal.

3. *Community Service Programs* like Stonegate, Masonic Home, Day Care Center, and Convalescent Homes are a strong plus. We are alone in offering students a term off from athletics for this sort of activity. Care of the ill and aged can touch the adolescent heart as contact with their peers may not.

4. Other programs putting students in other than academic situations are all valuable. Examples: *News, Brief, Press Club,* Gold Key, Student Tutoring, etc. (I'm not sure about Junior Achievement and some of the other money-making ventures.)

5. Our "Alternate Exercise Program" in a.m. or p.m. hours for those wishing to pursue worthy projects in the arts or community service is a strong incentive for the kind of flexibility in curriculum that offers kids good choices.

6. Our *programs in the arts, drama and club athletics* offer kids the chance to excel in non-academic enterprises requiring collaboration, patience, interdependence, and humor — all without the intense competition characterizing too many hours in a student's life.

7. The large number of *women faculty* and the rather astonishing number of *young faculty* (contrasted with our fellow schools) at CRH give us attitudinal advantages and freedoms from traditions not always found in our sister schools.

Uncertain Areas

1. Despite skepticism that the didactic approach to M.E. works, most schools offer at least as wide a variety as CRH does of courses in religion, philosophy, ethics, decision-making, current dilemmas, etc. How good are our course offerings? I suspect, from the constant changes they undergo, that they are not yet the best. Who has the best? Ellie Drury feels we should join Andover in trying to evaluate what is being done at all our schools so that we take advantage of others' experience in an area not often successfully approached in the classroom.

2. *House Counselors* at CRH are a new and relatively untried force in the M.E. picture. We do offer them some preliminary training (minimal) and do make our hopes and expectations fairly clear. Other schools do a lot more with their proctors, prefects, or Sixth Formers during pre-school orientation and afterwards. It's possible that "tradition" can be a negative here, but I suspect that we are on the inexperienced side, and therefore less effective than we might be.

3. *Youth* of Faculty, *Diversity* of both Faculty and Student body are potentially "iffy": unsure role models, too many cultural traditions not always unanimous in valuing God, honesty, wealth, courtesy, possessions, friends, patriotism, etc. Though pluralism is part of the real world, it complicates any plan for M.E. at a residential school like CRH.

Negative Areas on the CRH Scene

1. *Counseling Support* at CRH seems minimal in contrast to that in several of our sister schools. Our Doctor, Consultant, and Team hardly comprise one full-time person. Several other schools had more support per student. I do not argue for a single or two full-time persons; having available several persons of various ages, different sexes, is probably a plus. It's the hours per day or week of availability that matter, and I believe we are not providing enough trained help.

2. *Chapel-Religious-Spiritual* nourishment at CRH is admittedly undergoing reestablishment under trying circumstances. Schools which had not gone so far away from formalized religious offerings haven't had so far to come back to them. We are behind our sister schools.

3. *Lack of Tradition* at CRH as the community "reshapes" under a new flag, so to speak. Conflicts in traditions of Choate and Rosemary Hall ways of doing things in housing, student advising, faculty participation in three modes of life; the relatively large turnover in faculty and its youth; the expansion of the community from 600 to over a thousand students and faculty — all these and other factors have created a community where the questions "How are things done here?", or "What happens if...?", or "What is the philosophy of the school toward...?" still can receive too varied answers. We must continue to proclaim the philosophy of the new coeducational school loudly and often.

4. *Faculty role modeling*, at CRH as at all other schools, is uneven. Greatest cause of problems? Perhaps faculty too concerned with their own area or special enthusiasm to be effective models of tolerance, collaboration, good humor, etc. In the daily competition for student time, the zeal of these persons may constitute a major threat to the sense of community so necessary to helping kids see all things in perspective.

5. *Faculty Housing*, which in too many cases at CRH means a lack of privacy that leads to all kinds of exhaustion, loss of dignity, loss of self-confidence. The annual mini-exodus of qualified faculty members from CRH dormitories and those of other schools to day schools or other careers suggests that we should balance our "open door" policies with some officially sanctioned "closed door" policies. The health, happiness, and stability of our faculty may require them.

Good Ideas from Other Schools as They Might be Applied to CRH.

1. Changes at CRH designed to foster M.E. should be approached *indirectly*, not through the Academic Committee, Deans and Heads, etc. Faculty might be asked, for example, to set "maturity" as an objective for students and curriculum. Invite individuals to spell out ways and means of helping students achieve it. Avoid stressing term "moral education" and "change."

2. CRH needs to spell out in specific terms the philosophical or "character" goals we have for students. The declaration in the NEASC self-evaluation can be reworked for brevity and clarity. What qualities do we honor most? Responsibility? Maturity?

Fairness? Compassion? We need to be more clearly aware so that we can provide more specific situations to teach those values.

3. "There can be no moral growth without broken rules." We need rules — perhaps slightly uncomfortable (unrealistic) ones. The super-virtuous student who never breaks rules does not grow morally.

4. St. Paul's has a regular Monday luncheon involving the Rector, Vice-Rectors, Counselor, and Doctor to discuss "students with hurts." The regular tracking and follow-up has been effective.

5. Hotchkiss faculty, three times each year, discusses every student! These meetings require five days! Risks of categorizing students are apparently not great. Exeter and Deerfield expressed feelings that such a discussion violated a kid's privacy. Hotchkiss reply: Who cares about privacy in a caring and supportive community? Regular weekly meeting of M.D., Dean of Students, Head, etc., are devoted to following kids in trouble and keeping them in sight.

6. "Math Anxiety Classes" at Deerfield proved remarkably effective. Counselor ran them with permission of math teachers during regular math class periods.

7. Workshops for proctors at several schools: small groups, run by counselors, wide range of topics such as "helping skills."

8. Heath stressed the importance of play, especially when involves both kids and adults on levels chosen by the adolescents. Softball tournament, Project Adventure, all these are very sound.

9. A central, attractive faculty lounge and gathering place is essential. The Archbold location would be ideal.

III. Recommendations for the Future

Summary and Recommended Means to Foster M.E. at CRH

CRH should make an effort to redirect enough time and effort from Academic Education to Character Education to strike a new balance between them. As in many other schools, our past assumption may well have been that if we give graduates a good academic training, good character will automatically follow. There is much evidence to suggest the reverse, that students with sound values and high moral senses will happily and successfully see to their own education, even long after college years.

We should acknowledge the benefits emerging from the affiliation and coordination struggles of the recent past. Significant results of those battles include:

a) a relatively open attitude toward change,
b) a large number of students involved in decision-making,
c) a large number of young faculty,
d) a large number of women faculty whose views and positions are widely respected.

We should affirm to the faculty the relatively large number of ways in which we are offering our students good opportunities for M.E. To the four points listed above can be added mention of School and Community Service Programs and the dimensions they offer for encouraging compassion and service; arts and athletic programs and what they can mean in teaching collaboration and sportsmanship, the entire disciplinary system and the efforts of both faculty and students to discover and implement the concept of fairness. In all these areas, let there be honest thought and talk about the moral issues and values involved. It is not enough to assume that sports teach sportsmanship. Too often they teach quite the opposite, as we all know. Let the CRH Community talk about the values we most wish to teach.

To Improve Faculty Role Modeling

Since Moral Education is a forbiddingly heavy topic, we propose as light as possible a means of approaching it with the faculty. We suggest the format of a faculty meeting with a dramatized presentation of a particular issue, followed by a small group discussion of the issue raised by the skit or role playing. Any number of situations or problems could be approached in this manner, of which several are suggested below. The cooperation of Terry Ortwein, Rod Skinner, and those experienced or interested in dramatized role playing will be vital, of course. It is our hope that faculty will be able to see in the skits the kinds of situations in which they frequently find themselves, inevitably as role models. With imagination and practice, we should be able to portray good and bad role models in a wide variety of situations; we can also dramatize some existing unresolved problems in the CRH community that need faculty discussion. A few examples will illustrate — the first two below involving role modeling, the last three touching existing problems:

1. *Confrontation Scenes.* Teaching people to play ostrich is bad M.E. Yet confrontations can be embarrassing or worse. Innumerable situations involving faculty/student, faculty/faculty, adult/adolescent relationships can be imagined, such as:

> How does one faculty member (A) convey to another (B) the frequent criticisms (A) has heard from students about (B)'s relentless use of sarcasm in class?

How does a student convey to a teacher his resentment at the teacher's obvious favoritism toward another student?

2. *The "Put down,"* popular social weapon of our day, can leave cruel and lasting wounds. Whether it be one teacher criticizing another or another's subject area, especially if to students, or any number of classroom situations, the put down is inevitably an uncaring, insensitive act. Some are deliberate, others perhaps no more than thoughtless. Both can be effectively dramatized, their consequences discussed.

3. *Competition.* Some of the undesirable products of excessive competition among students (perhaps even within the faculty) include plagiarism, partying, and self-centeredness. In the press to get ahead, who can pause to help another? What about stealing and vandalism?

4. *Job-Family Demands* facing faculty. What should the faculty member's response be when a student seeking math help knocks on the door at the very moment when a spouse or child needs, with equal urgency, that adult's presence?

5. *Dean-Counselor Conflict.* Situations have arisen, and many can easily be envisioned, where a student's or the community's welfare can be jeapardized by inadequate communication between a counselor exercising the privilege of confidentiality and a dean seeking to treat a disciplinary matter fairly. How can the two adults be better informed? What are the limits of confidentiality?

Adult Support Group

The "Skits and Talks" approach seeks to strengthen faculty role modeling and to address some existing problems. For those interested, a more sustained effort to improve the quality of adult life and to achieve human renewal can be made through establishment of a voluntary adult group, certainly involving spouses and perhaps using a professional consultant. "Men's groups," "women's groups," "adult support groups" operate across the country offering nonthreatening processes of self-discovery. The sharing of common perceptions and anxieties can be profoundly supportive. A group to consider carefully the impact of institutional life upon marrige, for example, might not only benefit its participants personally, but might eventually offer suggestions of great value to the institution and its employees in the future.

Marriage is not the only topic such a group might address. Personal and professional growth, financial security, adult participation in the community beyond the campus confines are others. Lest the relationship between an adult support group and Moral Education at CRH be missed, let it be said that effective role models are courageous rather than insecure persons, men and women who are personally content with their image of themselves and their position within an institution or in the broad scheme of life. To strengthen the role models we place before students is to strengthen M.E. at CRH.

Day of Reflection

October 17 has been designated on the calendar as a Day of Reflection. Ellie Drury has prepared a memorandum which describes the intent, program, and problems of the proposed Day. With good management and a share of luck, the Day could substantially encourage the kind of attitudes we consider those of a moral person: caring, sensitive, listening.

Needless to say, one Day of Reflection will not bring about a permanent change in the moral climate of an institution of the size and complexity of CRH. Sustained efforts and periodic pauses to focus attention on moral issues will be necessary to strike the new balance between academic and moral education which we deem desirable.

Douglas Heath's Visit

To assist the participants in the Exeter Institute in introducing some of the concepts of M.E. to the CRH faculty and to stimulate faculty thought and interest, we have retained Doug Heath for October 6. He will speak to the faculty at a special faculty meeting that evening (Friday) and remain on campus for at least part of Saturday morning to continue discussion with interested faculty, perhaps even to conduct a demonstration class illustrating his indirect methods of teaching values in a classroom situation.

SUMMARY

Thus we see an on-going program with four elements:

A. An exposition to the CRH community (perhaps via this report) of our intentions, with a strong affirmation of all we seem to being doing right.

B. "Skits and Talks" Faculty Meetings — several each year.

C. Adult support Group or Groups — voluntary and continuing.

D. Day of Reflection — to be repeated if experience suggests.

ALSO PUBLISHED BY
The Phillips Exeter Academy Press

Respecting the Pupil: Essays on Teaching Able Students by Members of the Faculty of Phillips Exeter Academy, Donald B. Cole and Robert H. Cornell, Editors. 1981.